User-Centred Engineering

Michael Richter • Markus Flückiger

User-Centred Engineering

Creating Products for Humans

 Springer

Michael Richter
Markus Flückiger
Zühlke Engineering AG
Schlieren
Switzerland

ISBN 978-3-662-51573-0   ISBN 978-3-662-43989-0 (eBook)
DOI 10.1007/978-3-662-43989-0
Springer Heidelberg New York Dordrecht London

Printed on acid-free paper

Springer is part of Springer Science+Business Media (www.springer.com)

Foreword

This book is aimed first and foremost at people involved in software and product development – product managers, project managers, consultants and analysts, who face the major challenge of developing highly useful and usable products. Our objective is to provide you with an expert overview of the subject. You will find answers to the following questions:

- What is user-centred engineering?
- How do user-centred activities fit into the development process?
- How do I schedule user-centred techniques and what is the process involved?
- What results will I obtain and how can I verify them?
- How can I establish a user-centric culture within my business?
- What related fields are there and where can I find further information?

However, you *won't* find in this book:

- Rules, adherence to which guarantees great user experiences
- Cookbook instructions to improve usability
- User interface guidelines for developers
- Theory which has no practical application

We hope also to provide interested lay readers with an easily comprehensible introduction to the subject. As users of technical systems, we all have a choice – either we accept what is put in front of us or we don't. Of course it is not always possible to switch to a different product whenever we feel the need, but even then we can at least contribute to improving the existing one. The first step is to understand how this can be achieved.

Schlieren, Switzerland

Michael Richter
Markus Flückiger

Contents

Introduction

1

Space: the final frontier. These are the voyages of the Starship Enterprise. Captain's log, stardate 2200. The computer refuses to understand a word we say to it. Scotty has spent the last week trying in vain to get to grips with the new transporter controls. The tricorder continues to emit the same incomprehensible error message.

1.1   We Are All Users

Have you ever noticed how people on television always manage to interact with their technology effortlessly? We, by contrast, get tangled up in software, type in the wrong PIN number, get lost in airports and despair at ever understanding our latest gadget. From our day-to-day dealings with technical systems, we all have a rough idea of what a good user experience means. So let's start this introduction with some classic everyday hits and misses. You will no doubt recall similar situations, involving highly or poorly usable technical systems:

- The ticket machine which works perfectly, right up until you try to buy a ticket (and get a receipt) for tomorrow.
- The new digital video recorder which, at the press of a button, allows you to record the football match while you answer the door to the pizza guy. Or, hang on, was it a shortcut key? Now where did I put those instructions?
- The simplicity with which music can be downloaded from the web, sorted into playlists and listened to anywhere on a smartphone.
- Your telephone bill once you finally manage to book a cinema ticket for this evening's film using the new automated booking system.

Interactive products are an everyday fact of life. You may be one of those people who have simply come to accept that many systems are almost unusable, while

© Springer-Verlag Berlin Heidelberg 2014
M. Richter, M. Flückiger, *User-Centred Engineering*,
DOI 10.1007/978-3-662-43989-0_1

others are excellent. Is this just the luck of the draw? What factors determine whether a product makes it very easy, hard or impossible for us to do what we want to do? What options are available for systematically addressing these factors during the development process? It is questions like these which user-centred engineering aims to address.

1.2   The User Is Not Like Me

You have probably undergone the experience of writing an important piece of text and then passing it on to someone else to read. You will probably also have experienced how valuable that person's comments proved to be. Having been immersed in the relevant topic for so long, you will have found yourself unable to see things from the point of view of the uninitiated reader. Whilst you could simply have written the piece on your own, it would certainly not have been as good as it was after incorporating your colleague's feedback.

Developing software or an interactive product is (in the vast majority of cases) more complicated than writing a piece of text. There is a significant disjunction between people working on a project and future users in two respects:

- The former are specialists who have been immersed in the relevant technology over a protracted period. Putting themselves in an unskilled user's shoes is no longer a simple matter.
- They are usually unfamiliar with the area in which the solution being developed will be used. It is the user here who is the expert. Developers will not have the time to familiarise themselves with the field, concepts and terminology, and certainly not with specific everyday processes, in any great detail.

Both of these factors point to the need for a user's perspective to enable the creation of an appropriate solution. User-centred engineering deals principally with methods for systematically incorporating the user perspective into the development process.

Background: Perspective Taking

In psychology, *perspective taking* describes the ability to understand a particular circumstance from someone else's point of view. Perspective taking develops during childhood. The ability to take another's perspective varies between individuals and over the course of our lives. This is not merely a question of being able to put yourself in someone else's shoes. Recognising the need for perspective taking, analysing a situation from another person's point of view and applying the resulting insights are also of vital importance.

1.3   What Is User-Centred Engineering?

Everything should be made as simple as possible, but no simpler. (Albert Einstein)

A User-Centred Approach

A product can be easy or difficult to use, it can be complicated or intuitive, understandable or incomprehensible, efficient or cumbersome, engaging or dispiriting, it can support the way we work and think – or not.

In the last decades, several fields have evolved that encompass a user-centred approach:

- Human Computer Interaction (HCI)
- Human Factors
- Interaction Design
- Usability Engineering
- User-centred Design (UCD)
- User Experience (UX)

We will show some differences in the focus of these disciplines throughout this book. However, what they all have in common is the goal to systematically develop and improve products for the people who use them.

Usability: More than Just the Quality of the User Interface

Usability has become a familiar term in everyday conversation, the media and in product descriptions. There are many different definitions of usability and it is not our aim here to come up with another set of formally correct, generally applicable concepts. To put this book into its proper context, however, we do need to define some terms.

Usability is sometimes understood in a narrow sense to mean a measure of the quality of user interface design. Quality criteria include the arrangement of control elements, the number of clicks required or the comprehensibility of labels and dialogs displayed.

But there is more to it than that. The usability of a system has to be assessed in the context of its use. Software applications and products exhibit good usability if the intended users are able to learn how to use them easily, are able to use them effectively and are able to achieve their objectives and perform their intended tasks satisfactorily.

A good illustration of the difference between a narrower and a broader understanding of usability is the huge popularity of texting (SMS) following the advent of the mobile phone. It is indisputably the case that numeric keypads on mobile phones were not designed for composing text. Indeed many users found composing messages using the keypad somewhat cumbersome. In the narrower sense, the

Fig. 1.1 Usability means how well users can employ a tool in their context to perform the tasks they wish to perform

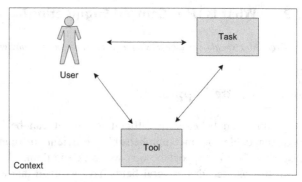

user interface was sub-optimal for these users. Looked at in the round, however, the application offered them exactly what they wanted – it enabled them to send short messages simply and efficiently. The system offered good support for the user's objective. In other words, the application as a whole exhibited good usability. As this example makes clear, to consider the user interface alone would be to adopt too narrow an approach.

Figure 1.1 shows the four principal components of a human-machine system.

A definition of usability in this broader sense has been laid down in an ISO standard. This definition is frequently quoted and you should therefore be familiar with it. ISO standard 9241-11 defines usability as "the extent to which a product can be used by specified users to achieve specified goals with effectiveness, efficiency and satisfaction in a specified context of use" [ISO 98].

From this definition, it follows that the widely-held view that usability is purely a product characteristic is incorrect. A very simple illustration: the usability of a hammer for driving in a nail may be very good, but it's pretty poor if the task at hand is to screw in a screw. Usability means how well users can employ a tool in their environment to perform the tasks they wish to perform. When designing a new product, that product needs to be adapted to the world of the user. Figure 1.2 illustrates the need to consider a number of consecutive levels when addressing usability. A similar approach can be found in [Garrett 10].

It follows that optimising the user interface alone is not sufficient to produce a usable solution. The following tasks are essential:

- analysing the user, their tasks and the usage context
- specifying the range of functions and information required
- identifying optimum processes and procedures

This book will frequently refer to *processes* or workflows from the user's perspective: What is the optimal way for users to achieve the desired outcome, given their skills, habits, preferences and the concrete circumstances? Designing products that suit the daily needs of those that will be using them becomes much easier once the project team acts based on this broader sense of usability. An overview of user-centred activities when developing software or products can be found in Sect. 2.2.

Fig. 1.2 Optimising
usability means considering
more than just the user
interface; factors such as the
purpose and functionality of
the product also need to be
taken into account

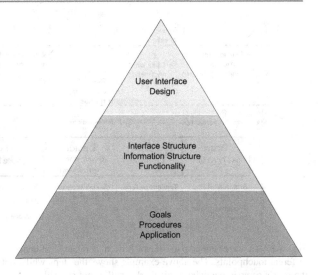

User Experience (UX): The User's Perception

The broader definition of usability in ISO 9241-11 points to the complex
interdependencies between context, users and the products users employ to perform
their tasks. Still the phrasing "usability of a product" puts the stress on the product
and the term *usability* itself evokes a very pragmatic and functional viewpoint on
the matter. While this may be a substantial improvement for many business
software packages, it doesn't appear sufficient for consumer products and smart
apps. Emotions, values, aesthetics, wit, and more can make the difference between
a bestseller and a shelf warmer.

The concept of the user's experience addresses these needs. Instead of creating a
pragmatic product for users, create a great experience for humans. A definition of
user experience has also been laid down in an ISO standard. ISO 9241-210 defines
user experience as "a person's perceptions and responses that result from the use or
anticipated use of a product, system or service" [ISO 10]. The term strongly promotes
adopting the users' perspective and leaving pure functional considerations.

- User experience looks at the overall experience of using a service or product. It
  also applies to experiences with non-technical systems such as shopping centres,
  museums, libraries, trade shows and similar institutions.
- The focus is not confined to functional factors, but also involves emotional
  factors concerning design and aesthetics which can increase the pleasure users
  derive from using a product.
- UX also encompasses non-product factors. In particular, it aims to improve the
  experience wherever the user comes into contact with the company (*customer
  touchpoints*), for example prior to and after using a product. This includes

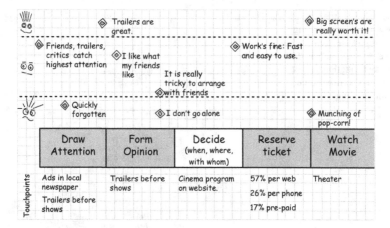

◈ Trailers are great.				◈ Big screen's are really worth it!
◈ Friends, trailers, critics catch highest attention	◈ I like what my friends like		◈ Work's fine: Fast and easy to use.	
		◈ It is really tricky to arrange with friends		
◈ Quickly forgotten		◈ I don't go alone		◈ Munching of pop-corn!

Draw Attention	Form Opinion	Decide (when, where, with whom)	Reserve ticket	Watch Movie
Ads in local newspaper	Trailers before shows	Cinema program on website.	57% per web	Theater
Trailers before shows			26% per phone	
			17% pre-paid	

(left axis label: Touchpoints)

Fig. 1.3 An experience map shows how a company influences customer experience across different touchpoints. The above example shows the steps whilst obtaining a cinema ticket from the user's perspective, where this works well or not so well

information collection, support whilst placing an order or making a purchase and seeking support in the event of problems.

- The idea of providing a positive experience for the customer as a (potential) purchaser (**customer experience**) is closely connected with service marketing, the aim of which is likewise to provide customers with an ideal experience. To achieve this, internal processes need to be aligned according to customer needs. Figure 1.3 shows an example of an experience map, a way of modelling the customer's journey before, during and after using a product or service.

In looking at the overall experience of dealing with a product, the concept of user experience also has much to say about product design, user interface design and associated processes. A detailed treatment containing many useful examples can be found in the book *Sketching User Experiences* [Buxton 07].

User-Centred Engineering: Reduction to the Essential

User-centred engineering encompasses materials and techniques for achieving the desired user experience when developing new software or products. This includes determining who exactly makes up the user group, analysing workflows, scoping the ideal functionality and specifying the basic design for a suitable user interface.

One important goal is the avoidance of unnecessary complexity and the reduction of a product's functionality to what is, for the user, the ideal minimum. A technical system should assist the user to the best possible extent in achieving his or her objectives and should be designed with exactly this in mind. This reduction to the essential doesn't just happen of its own accord and project teams need to contain people who possess the relevant skills. The cost and work involved is quickly repaid when it comes to implementation.

Food for Thought

Imagine a toaster which also makes fried eggs. Which target group does this product address?

(a) Toast lovers
(b) Fried egg lovers
(c) Both groups – toast lovers and fried egg lovers
(d) The subset of toast and egg lovers who prefer to enjoy their morning toast with a fried egg.

Bonus question: What's the best way of matching toasting time to frying time?

The thought experiment above is intended to illustrate another important issue – products are frequently equipped with a lot of different features with the aim of attracting a lot of different purchasers. But more functionality generally comes at a price – it makes operating the product more complex. It is essential that this additional complexity does not exceed the benefit as perceived by the user, otherwise users will not accept the product or will switch to a competitor product – the target group of potential users will be reduced, rather than increased. User-centred engineering, when applied consistently, flags up such targeting conflicts at the start of the product development process. See also the case study in Sect. 6.3.

Areas Where User-Centred Engineering Can Be Applied

User-centred engineering as described in this book applies wherever users are involved with technical systems. This encompasses both workplace software and products used for leisure purposes. This book tends to focus on systems with a graphical user interface (GUI) and the development of software applications and products with software-based user interfaces. In view of the many degrees of freedom and the complexity inherent in modern software development, we see this as being the point at which a user-centric approach exerts the maximum effect. The methods and principles described can, however, readily be used to optimise the user experience of interactive voice response systems, physical controls, signage or any other technical system.

When Humans and Products Don't Fit

Food for Thought

Are you involved in developing software or products? If yes, how do you ensure that your products match the needs of the people who use them?

The question above may sound trite. But then, how do you know what your users really need? Did they evaluate your products? Tracing the symptoms of a mismatch back to their cause is not always a simple matter. As a result, companies may choose to up their marketing spend rather than undertaking user-centred measures. The following list shows some of these symptoms:

- Staff are not working at the hoped-for pace when using the system.
- Induction and user training are very time-consuming.
- There is a noticeable drop in the quality of the work produced.
- The hotline is experiencing excessive demand.
- Increase of complaints and bad press in social networks.
- Staff are minimising the activities they carry out using the system. Workflows are dealt with using alternative methods.
- Operating procedures are being circumvented and safety measures ignored.
- There are repeated cases of 'user error' leading to losses (accidents, data loss, commercial losses).
- Higher rate of returns by dissatisfied customers.
- Customers are reluctant to upgrade to the new product.
- Customers switch to competitor's products.

1.4   Lessons from History

To understand the context of user-centred engineering as a discipline, it is worth looking at some of the major milestones and people who have made key contributions to the creation and popularisation of the field:

- In the fifteenth century, Leonardo da Vinci placed an understanding of people at the heart of the process of developing new technologies. His ideas have exerted a lasting influence on science and technology.
- In the 1940s, the military, and the US military in particular, invested in optimising human-machine interfaces for complex systems. The result was the development of a field of study examining the effects of **human factors** in the use of technology.
- In 1957, the first issue of *Ergonomics* was published. It was this journal which triggered the international diffusion of **ergonomics** as an academic discipline concerned with the relationship between man and his work.
- In 1970, Brian Shackel founded UK research institute HUSAT (*Human Sciences and Advanced Technology*). The study of communication between man and computers (**human-computer interaction** or *HCI*) became a recognised academic discipline.
- In the mid 1980s, the systematic study of human-computer interaction was given new impetus by the increased prevalence of computers in the workplace and the advent of **software ergonomics**. A wide range of ground-breaking publications were produced in the Germanophone world in particular.

- In 1988, Donald Norman published his classic work *The Psychology of Everyday Things* [Norman 88]. The book powerfully illustrates the importance of psychological factors when developing technical systems.
- In 1993, Jakob Nielsen published *Usability Engineering* [Nielsen 93]. The book describes the use of usability techniques within a systematic process and is considered to have pioneered the user-centric approach.
- In 1996, user-centred concepts became part of the international standard series ISO 9241. The standard soon evolved to an important reference in the field. Since its revision in 2006 it is named "Ergonomics of Human System Interaction" and contains a human-centred process when developing new systems [ISO 1996–2014].
- During the internet boom of the late 1990s, a lot of companies focused their energies on the web. Demand for the production of user-friendly websites and applications exploded. *Web usability* was the new buzzword.
- In the new millennium, increasing digitisation of content such as music, photos and video, and the general affordability of web devices and broadband connections led to further change. Computers started to be used for work, communication and entertainment, and became everyday objects. Web 2.0 and **social media** sites resulted in more and faster sharing of content and information. New technologies with revolutionary human-computer interaction concepts became suitable for everyday use and started to achieve market penetration. User experience became an important factor for companies in differentiating themselves and their products from their competitors.
- In 2007, Apple unveiled the *iPhone*. The device introduced revolutionary intuitive interaction techniques and set a new standard for user-friendliness in the mobile product and application field. The related ability to install small applications (**Apps**) on mobile devices has achieved enormous popularity. The ease of use of the iPhone and other smartphones ushered in a new era for information technology.
- Since then, smartphones, tablets and mobile applications are changing the way we live, work and communicate. Today, manifold new technologies and sensors in mobile devices promise additional novel interactions and applications. The **mobile user experience** that companies deliver with their products and applications is becoming more and more crucial for their success (see also Sect. 8.5).

User-Centred Engineering

2

To set out a one-size-fits-all user-centred engineering procedure suitable for all of the many different situations you are likely to meet is, in our opinion, impossible. Similarly, it is not our aim to provide a recipe book, containing step-by-step instructions on how to apply user-centred techniques. The chapters which follow are instead intended to assist you in understanding how user-centred engineering can be applied during software and product development in practice, how key user-centred techniques actually operate, how they can be planned within your project and what points you need to watch out for.

This chapter provides an overview of the relationship between various user-centred techniques and how they are integrated into common software development processes. The next chapter describes individual techniques in more detail.

2.1 Software Engineering: The Forgotten User?

Software Development Processes

According to an oft-quoted study by the Standish Group, *incomplete requirements* and *lack of user involvement* are among the leading reasons why software projects fail [Standish Group 94–14]. Recent approaches aspire to provide a remedy for this problem. Most modern process frameworks accord a high priority to requirements analysis and requirements management.

The *Unified Process,* an established software development process, defines **requirements** as one of six primary disciplines of software engineering (see Table 2.1).

The *Requirements* discipline covers those activities concerned with identifying, documenting and managing the various stakeholders' requirements (see "Background: Requirements Engineering"). As key stakeholders, users play a central role. More practical information about the unified process can be found in [Kroll et al. 03].

© Springer-Verlag Berlin Heidelberg 2014
M. Richter, M. Flückiger, *User-Centred Engineering*,
DOI 10.1007/978-3-662-43989-0_2

Table 2.1 The six primary software engineering disciplines in the Unified Process (source: IBM Rational Unified Process®). Most user-centred activities can be found in the *Business Modelling* and *Requirements* disciplines

Discipline	Purpose
Business modelling	To understand the structure and the dynamics, current problems and improvement potentials of the target organisation
	To ensure that customers, users, and developers have a common understanding of the target organisation
Requirements	To establish and maintain agreement with stakeholders on what the system should do
	To provide system developers with a better understanding of the requirements
	To define the boundaries of the system
	To provide a basis for planning as well as cost and time estimation to develop the system
	To define a user interface for the system, focusing on the needs and goals of the users
Analysis & design	Transforming the requirements into a design of the system-to-be
	To evolve a robust architecture for the system
Implementation	Defining the organization of the code, implementing classes and objects, testing the developed components and integrating the results into an executable system
Test	Validating the software product functions as designed and that the requirements have been implemented appropriately
Deployment	Ensuring that the software product is available for its end users

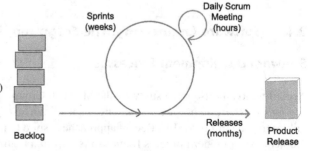

Fig. 2.1 In Scrum, the project team transforms the top priority requirements from the backlog (work to do) in short iterations, called sprints, into product releases. Each sprint is a feedback cycle

Agile methods such as Scrum rely on even more communication and tighter feedback cycles (compare Fig. 2.1) between the various parties involved in software development. Short iterations allow fast feedback on a running product already in early stages of development (see also "Background: Agile Software Development"). For details about Scrum we refer you to the Scrum Guide® [Schwaber et al. 91–13].

Modern software development processes thus fulfil many essential conditions for performing user-centred activities:

- User needs are identified during requirements analysis.
- Requirements are described from a user perspective and taken forward into the development process.
- An iterative approach permits continuous monitoring and refinement of results with customers and users.
- A number of best practices from the usability engineering field, such as user interface storyboards for visualising dialog flows, personas for characterising users and the creation of prototype GUIs, are explicitly mentioned in many procedural descriptions.

Can we therefore assume that users and user requirements are already being taken into account on a systematic basis in product development in general and user interface design in particular? Does this mean that our problem is solved? Reality suggests otherwise. In many projects, the user interface is produced by developers alone with no external assistance. Appropriate methods and techniques for involving end users are often lacking. Many projects view a user-centric approach as optional or as creating additional work and therefore omit such activities.

Background: Agile Software Development

Agile methodologies involve breaking software development down into short cycles, known as iterations, of usually between two and four weeks. The result of each iteration is a concrete, tested (including with customers) sub-product. Where the functionality so far implemented permits, this product can potentially also be shipped.

An iteration in particular is a learning process. To this end, the team, together with customers, defines what exactly is to be developed, implements and tests the agreed software and then reflects on the results and the process and institutes any necessary improvements. This procedure ensures that the project team familiarises itself with the product to be developed and the technologies employed and learns how to work as a team.

Agile teams therefore strive to minimise the time between firming up the specification – in direct consultation with customers rather than via documents – and actual development. The specification is thus produced on the basis of insights obtained from the sub-products developed, a better understanding of the problem and optimised teamwork. The project team is constantly reassessing how the best possible product can be achieved with remaining resources.

Agile principles were originally defined in the *Manifesto for Agile Software Development* [Beck et al. 01]:

- Communication between those involved (including the end user) is prioritised over defining processes and tools.
- Working software is considered more important than comprehensive documentation.
- Collaboration with the customer is more important than contract negotiations.
- Responding to change is prioritised over following a plan.

The philosophy pursued by agile methodologies is firmly oriented towards human thought processes and teamwork and thus promises to increase software development productivity.

User-Centred Process Models

Conversely, process models which describe how user-centred techniques are applied have been around for a good 20 years. We refer you to some excellent integrated user-oriented models by various prominent experts in the field:

- *The Usability Engineering Lifecycle* by Deborah Mayhew [Mayhew 99] describes the relationship between usability techniques across the product lifecycle as a whole during development of a new solution. Mayhew illustrates how user requirements are used to determine usability goals and implemented in user interface designs, which are in turn tested with users.
- *Contextual Design* by Hugh Beyer and Karen Holtzblatt [Beyer et al. 98] is a user-oriented design process. This involves a more detailed analysis of users and the user environment and illustrates how the information obtained can be incorporated into the development process. This process gives rise to the contextual inquiry method (cf. Sect. 3.1).
- *Goal Directed Design* by Alan Cooper [Cooper et al. 07] describes a procedure for modelling user requirements and implementing them within an appropriate interaction design. Cooper's approach to designing new solutions is oriented towards the user's underlying goals. To portray relevant user characteristics and needs, Cooper introduces the use of archetypal users (personas – see Sect. 3.2).

A process model for *user-centred design for interactive systems* has even been set out in an ISO standard (ISO 9241-210). Figure 2.2 shows the key process steps. A more detailed description of these steps is contained in ISO [10].

Adopting these approaches will undoubtedly produce better software and products. But there's no getting away from the fact that they do not integrate well with common software and product development processes. This aloofness may be partly to blame for the fact that the involvement of end users is viewed by many clients and project team members as an expensive, time-consuming add-on to existing processes.

If you need to carry out a project in accordance with an existing model or using a specific development process (because your company requires it or simply because you find that it offers many benefits), how can you integrate user-centred methods into that model or process? Should you analyse required workflows by applying business modelling or user observation? Would you be better using scenarios, user stories or use cases for your specification? At what point should you be testing your new solution with users and with how many? The aim of the next chapter is to assist you with these and similar issues.

Fig. 2.2 ISO standard 9241-210 defines the steps which need to be adhered to for user-centred design of interactive systems. A proposal for a new solution meets requirements only once it has been successfully evaluated with users

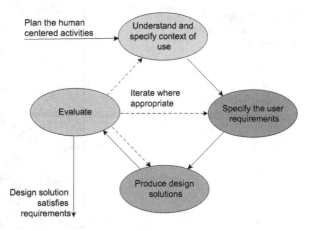

The Best of Both Worlds

Experience obtained over the course of many different projects has shown us that user-centred activities can indeed be seamlessly integrated into common software and product development processes and that this offers many benefits. Application of user-centred techniques for *requirements engineering*, for example, has in practice proven to be extremely successful. Firstly it means that user requirements are considered systematically during analysis; secondly it makes it possible to ensure that these requirements actually get implemented. The result is a solution which is oriented towards the actual purpose for which it is used.

In taking such an integrated viewpoint, it is not enough to simply follow procedures unthinkingly. The principles on which these two different worlds are based need to be understood and given due consideration.

Background: Requirements Engineering
Requirements Engineering is concerned with ensuring that the needs of users, the client and other stakeholders are dealt with, managed and communicated in such a way as to enable the project team to create an appropriate solution. A key factor for ensuring a successful project is having goals which have been agreed by and for which responsibility is borne by all stakeholders. The analyst can build on this in identifying quality requirements and in scoping the functionality and modelling the behaviour of the solution. A good overview of this topic can be found in [Robertson et al. 12].

2.2   Overview: User-Centred Techniques in Context

Note: This section describes how user-centred techniques can be integrated into commonly used software engineering models. It is intended as an overview for the experienced reader. For readers new to this topic, we recommend first familiarising

Fig. 2.3 Principle task areas during product and system development

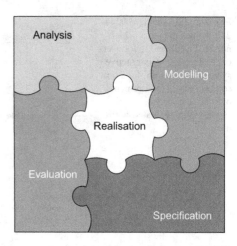

yourself with the individual techniques and concepts in the next chapter (The 7 ± 2 most important user-centred techniques).

Core software and product development tasks can be roughly divided into five broad areas. This subdivision facilitates understanding of the purpose and objectives of the techniques employed and of the results which the work aims to achieve. They are development process-independent. Figure 2.3 shows an overview of these task areas.

From a user-centric point of view, each area can be seen to have a different objective.

- *Analysis:* Understanding the user and context
- *Modelling:* Designing and optimising a suitable solution
- *Specification:* Moving the solution forward into development
- *Realisation:* Supporting implementation of the solution
- *Evaluation:* Testing the results with users

These task areas do not represent a chronological sequence. It may, for example, be productive to start by evaluating an existing system before starting work on modelling a new solution. Alternatively, it may be helpful to produce an initial model to aid analysis. In practice a team may even work in parallel in several areas. The chronological relationship between these areas will be discussed in more detail in Chap. 4.

Below, we discuss approaches and techniques derived both from software engineering and from user-centred process models and how these approaches and techniques fit together within an integrated process. Details of individual techniques are discussed in the next chapter.

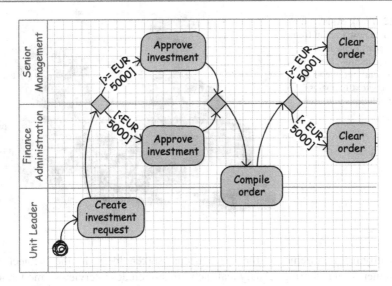

Fig. 2.4 Model of a sample business process for hardware procurement

Analysing Users and Context

At the start of any new project, the project team is faced with the challenge of planning a new solution without knowing exactly what it will be used for, what features it should offer or who will use it.

Quite commonly, the starting point might be a business driver. In the following example project a manager eventually decided that the way of how hardware was procured in his division just did cause too much trouble and that this should change.

Business analysis/business modelling analyses the business processes into which the new solution will be integrated. Due consideration also needs to be given to the fact that the introduction of a new solution will generally itself modify these processes. Figure 2.4 shows a segment of one such business process.

A detailed description of the activities involved in analysis and modelling is beyond the scope of this book. What matters here is that business processes help establishing the framework for a new solution – which points and processes within the business will be affected, for example, which tasks and activities are performed at these points and how information flows and collaboration occurs between these various points. This information can be used to define the tasks for which the new system is to be used from a business point of view.

In addition to formal business processes, a solid understanding of the new solution's users and how it will actual be used in the course of day-to-day business is also essential. User-centred engineering fleshes out formal processes from business modelling with specific details of day-to-day operations and abstract business roles with the characteristics and capabilities of the actual people behind these roles.

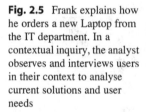
Fig. 2.5 Frank explains how he orders a new Laptop from the IT department. In a contextual inquiry, the analyst observes and interviews users in their context to analyse current solutions and user needs

Identifying requirements for the various stakeholders is the subject of requirements engineering. Analytical activities include interviews, moderated workshops and analysis of old systems and documentation. User-centred techniques are used to identify requirements from the user perspective and as such complement requirements engineering techniques.

Within this book, **contextual inquiry** (see Sect. 3.1) will be used as a representative example for other techniques ranging from observations, interviews and focus groups, to structured task analysis. The objective of these techniques is to understand user needs and context. Specific tasks, processes, patterns of behaviour and the usage environment are analysed, interpreted and documented by observing and interviewing users in situ. Figure 2.5 shows a situation from a contextual inquiry in our procurement process example.

Results are documented in the form of graphical models or natural language descriptions. Figure 2.6 shows the results of an on-site investigation of the procurement process depicted in Fig. 2.4. Compare the two results. Can you spot the differences?

Modelling an Appropriate Solution

Even for smaller applications, it is virtually impossible to design a system which fulfils every requirement right off the bat. A new system needs to be modelled from a range of perspectives, the specification needs to be firmed up gradually. Designs will be produced and feedback collected over a number of cycles. The team will model areas such as integration into business processes, how users work with the new system, and system functionality and behaviour.

Insights obtained by analysing users and context are applied using personas and scenarios (see Sect. 3.2).

Personas represent profiles of archetypal users, whilst **scenarios** describe working with the new system from the user's perspective. Personas and scenarios sum up

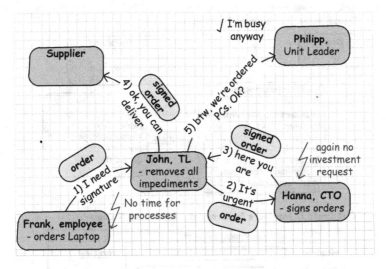

Fig. 2.6 Diagram of information flows derived by examining work in context

---

Usage Scenario 1: Ordering a new laptop

Jack works in the claims department of an insurance company. On a rainy Tuesday morning, while answering a call on the phone, his laptop freezed. The IT guys got him a spare laptop for the time being. In the evening, just before going home, Jack has five minutes to order the new one.

- Jack opens the service app on his tablet.
- Jack has three laptop models to choose from, he chooses the one with the biggest screen.
- Jack completes the order form, some fields are pre-filled (Jacks name, cost centre, costs)
- Jack marks the order as urgent and gives as reason «broken laptop» .
- In the distribution list, his boss Philipp is already entered as approver.
- Philipp receives an email that an urgent order needs his approval
- The IT centre receives a ticket that a laptop needs to be urgently replaced.

Fig. 2.7 A scenario describes the new solution from the perspective of a user

insights obtained from contextual inquiry in easily digestible form and are used as a basis for development work. Figure 2.7 shows an example scenario.

Personas and scenarios also provide a good basis for designing a **use case model** or **user stories** (see Sect. 3.5). This involves first outlining the functionality to be provided by the new solution, and then detailing the behaviour of the system, whilst ensuring that this behaviour is compatible with any quality requirements and constraints.

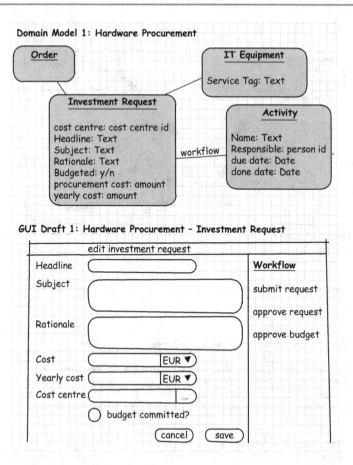

Fig. 2.8 Part of a domain model and corresponding GUI in our example procurement process

A precise understanding of the objects and data which will be represented within the system is essential for producing a user interface. These concepts and their relationships can be modelled using a *domain model*. A well designed domain model is a useful aid to producing a user interface. It shows which items are displayed and need to be entered and the relationships between these items. On the other hand, sketching out a user interface is useful to discuss the domain model with users and stakeholders and to validate if all items have been captured. Figure 2.8 shows a first draft of a sample domain model and the corresponding GUI.

Storyboards (see Sect. 3.3) can be used to present proposed solutions in an easily understood form. Storyboards visualize how life with a solution will be in the future - at least as much as the team can foretell. Storyboards are thus well suited for gathering feedback from users and managers for an early product idea.

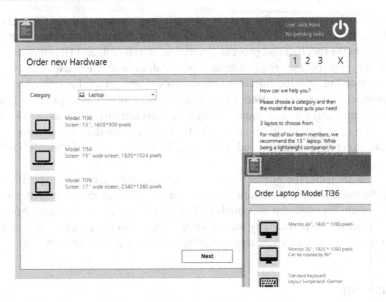

Fig. 2.9 GUI prototype after some more iterations: Special user interface prototyping tools allow to quickly sketch out a set of screens, connect them with each other, and by that create a clickable prototype users can use – at least a little

User interface prototyping (see Sect. 3.4) is used to further refine system behaviour. This involves putting together a rough implementation of initial dialogs and having them evaluated by selected users and other stakeholders. User interface prototypes provide stakeholders for the first time with an impression of the running application. They serve as an easily comprehensible language between users, the client and developers. Requirements become tangible!

Figure 2.9 shows a GUI prototype in our example after some more iterations.

Specifying

Once the concept for the intended solution has become sufficiently clear, it will be specified for development. In very formal projects, client and vendor use a requirements specification to pinpoint the technical content required to meet the terms of the contract. Use case specifications describe the system's behaviour. Alongside additional functional requirements, any non-functional requirements are also recorded (see Sect. 3.5 for further information about use cases and functional requirements). Requirements for the new solution are usually specified using structured documents or dedicated tools.

The boundary between the process of modelling the new solution and that of specifying it is somewhat fluid. Selected results from the modelling process are also employed in the specification process. Scenarios, storyboards and UI prototypes can also form part of the requirements specification and can help ensure that requirements fed into the implementation process are comprehensible, complete and precise. The **specification** ultimately consists of an amalgam of formal requirements notation and natural language descriptions such as a use case model, use case specifications, flow charts, a domain model, requirements sets, non-functional requirements and additional items such as storyboards and UI prototypes.

In agile projects, the emphasis is on direct communication. The specification should be the result of this communication and should be produced as contemporaneously with development as possible. The specification can be more informal. Agile projects are particularly suited to the use of demonstrative user-centred techniques, such as mock-ups and scenarios (cf. "User stories" in Sect. 3.5).

Realisation

In order to implement the solution, the specification needs to be transformed into a technical design. A software architecture needs to be designed and implemented. The developed components have to be tested. These tasks are the usual focus of software and product development process models.

Usability guidelines and **style guides** help to achieve a consistent, rules-compliant user interface design (see Sect. 3.6) and support implementation work.

User interface prototypes (see Sect. 3.4) form a useful basis for development. Modern software development processes and agile methodologies support an iterative approach consisting of short cycles in which variant solutions are produced and feedback is incorporated. This mentality is highly compatible with user-oriented approaches.

Evaluating the Results with Users

A major contribution of user-centred development is testing and optimising the product with users, even in an early state of the project. This may consist of components of the system which have already been implemented, prototypes or simple mock-ups. Oddly, popular software engineering models offer little assistance in this area, largely confining themselves to reviews and acceptance testing by the client. By contrast, a wide range of user-centred techniques for evaluating a system and the user's experience even in early stages of the process are available.

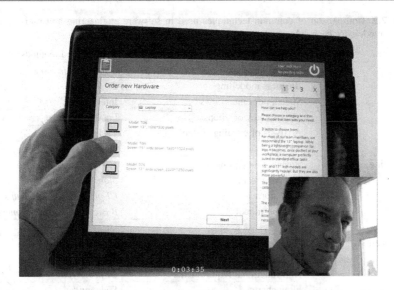

Fig. 2.10 Example video recording of a usability test: actual users solve tasks with the new solution. Problems and hidden requirements come to light

Formal **usability testing** involves placing users in a usability lab and observing how they work with the new application or prototype (see Sect. 3.7). Problems are recorded and used to identify areas for improvement. Usability testing can also be used to confirm conformity with requirements as part of acceptance testing. **Usability walkthroughs** are less formal and are suitable for testing and optimising early prototypes. Figure 2.10 shows a usability test situation with the GUI Prototype from our example.

Usability questionnaires (more on this in Sect. 3.8) can be used to obtain feedback on the usability of a new solution from a large number of users.

Finally, it is possible to test user interfaces using checklists or to have them tested by experts.

Summary of Techniques

Table 2.2 summarises the relationship between the techniques used in software engineering and the techniques used in user-centred process models. The italicised techniques are discussed in more detail in the following chapter.

Table 2.2 Comparison of common techniques used in software engineering and user-centred process models for each subtask

Task area	Software engineering	User-centred methods
Analysis	Business analysis	*Contextual inquiry*
	Business modelling	Observations
	Stakeholder interviews	Interviews
	Moderated workshops	Focus groups
	Analysis of existing systems	Task analysis
		Questionnaires
Modelling	Business modelling	*Personas and scenarios*
	Use case model	*Storyboards*
	User stories	*UI prototyping, mock-ups*
	Domain model	*Basic user interface concept*
	Glossary	
Specification	*Use case model*	*Scenarios*
	Use case specifications	*Storyboards*
	Non-functional requirements	*UI prototypes*
	Flow charts	*Style guides*
	Domain model	
	Requirements sets	
	User stories	
Realisation	Technical design	*Usability guidelines*
	Software architecture	*Style guides*
	Implementation	*UI prototypes*
Evaluation	Formal reviews	*Usability testing*
	Functional testing	Walkthroughs
	Acceptance testing	*Questionnaires*
		Checklists and heuristics
		Expert reviews

The 7 ± 2 Most Important User-Centred Techniques

3

In the previous chapter, we argued that user-centred activities can be seamlessly integrated into existing software engineering approaches and illustrated some of them in context. In this chapter we would like to explore 8[1] user-centred techniques in more detail. We are confident that this selection provides the reader with a comprehensive range of tools for developing highly useful products in a range of different situations. Table 3.1 summarises these eight methods and the principle purpose of each.

3.1   Aspects of Life: Contextual Inquiry

Hot features, cool technologies and seductive savings are out there waiting for you – all you have to do is reach out and grab them. Apparently, any problem in IT is simply a question of the right technology and has now, thanks to tablets, SOA and the cloud (insert IT marketing buzzword of choice here), been solved.

Contextual inquiry tackles the challenges not via the use of new technology, but via a solid understanding of future users and their activities and needs. Contextual

---

[1] An aside for interested readers: The number in the title is nothing other than the oft-quoted "magic number 7 ± 2". In 1956, psychologist George A. Miller published a paper on the limits of human information processing capacity [Miller 56]. It states that, on average, the human brain is able to evaluate a maximum of 5–9 comparable stimuli. This limit has been demonstrated in various experiments involving stimuli such as musical pitches, volumes, visual stimuli etc. The same number has also been identified in other studies. 7 ± 2 is the approximate number of pieces of information which someone can retain in their short term memory at one time. 7 ± 2 is the number of objects covered by the human attention span. Misunderstanding, coincidence or a law of nature? Whatever the case, ever since, the "magic number 7 ± 2" has been treated as a kind of fundamental constant. In the field of software ergonomics, it has been argued that the limits of human information processing capacity mean that, to be effective, selections should be limited to between around 5–9 different options.

© Springer-Verlag Berlin Heidelberg 2014
M. Richter, M. Flückiger, *User-Centred Engineering*,
DOI 10.1007/978-3-662-43989-0_3

Table 3.1 Overview of the most important user-centred techniques

Technique	Purpose
Contextual inquiry	Analysis of users and the context in which the new system will be used
Personas and scenarios	To model different user groups and usage from the user's perspective
Storyboards	To communicate selected processes using the new system
User interface prototyping	To clarify requirements and to optimise the user interface
Use cases and user stories	To take functional requirements forward into the development process
Guidelines and style guides	To define design principles
Usability testing	Evaluation of the new system by users
Questionnaires	To collect meaningful figures for analysing users and context or to evaluate a system or prototype

inquiry involves investigating the user's needs by observing their activities and asking questions.

Observing and Enquiring

A new software package to assist insurance agents is required. The project team pays a visit to some users in order to understand how the insurance agents go about their work. A key focus is the customer consultation, as the project specification involves producing software which will improve the quality of the advice provided. The analysts on the team take part in a number of customer consultations, observing and asking the agents questions about how the consultation proceeded. The analysts make a detailed record of which information is actually relevant and how agents use it to choose appropriate insurance products. The analysts also form a picture of some of the software applications currently being used by the insurance agents for tasks such as calculation, information storage and letter writing. The observation process enables the analysts to collect information which would not be brought to light simply by asking questions. This detailed information enables the project team to design a system suitable to the tasks performed by users.

Psychological research shows that people are not simply able to draw on much of the knowledge they employ in specific situations at will. Recording information of this type in an interview is not easy. The combination of observation and enquiry enables actual events to be recorded in detail and helps illuminate the reasons for and context of these events. This additional information is useful for determining the required information content of a system, identifying navigation patterns and scoping system functionality.

What Questions Need to Be Addressed?

The aim of contextual inquiry is to clarify selected questions. Worthwhile questions target how current products are used and the environment in which they are used. If you are undertaking further development for a satnav device, for example, it may be illuminating to explore the relative roles of the driver and passenger when heading off on holiday.

Before the analyst starts talking to users, the project team will sit down and look at what it needs to know in relation to the new system. Table 3.2 gives some more details on what to look for. There will of course also be questions which can't be answered using contextual inquiry, for example how much a customer will be willing to pay for a product (marketing and market research), whether a particular technology is appropriate (development) or how a business process should operate in principle (business modelling).

Table 3.2 Questions which can be investigated using contextual inquiry

Perspective	Question
Division of roles and communication	Typical division of roles
	Tasks and responsibilities
	Means of communication
	Purpose and content of communication
	Advantages of and problems associated with this division of roles
Strategies and procedures	How activities are performed
	Different ways of doing things
	Strengths and weaknesses
	Frequency, intensity and duration of an action
	Exceptional situations and errors, special cases
Artifacts	Documents, forms, tools, etc. used to perform the work
	Structure and information content
	Intended use
	Adaptation to individual requirements
	Non-intended use
	Advantages and problems when performing work
Cultural and social influences	People who exert influence
	Effects of social pressure, the exercise of power
	Codes of conduct
	Objectives, values and preferences
	Contradictory influences
	Problems and opportunities at the cultural level
Physical environment	How the space and workplace are arranged
	Available tools
	Routes and distances
	Effect on communication
	Potential for improvement

Fig. 3.1 Contextual inquiry
investigates various aspects
of the use of existing products
and systems in order to
illuminate the context of the
planned new solution in detail

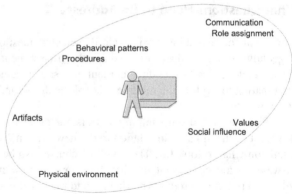

Contextual inquiry focuses on the activities of users and the use environment. Figure 3.1 presents five perspectives which can be recorded and documented using this method.

There are few environments in which it is possible to record the entire usage context in a single round of interviews. Experience shows that questioning tends to be broad to start with, and tends to become more specific and more tightly focused over the course of the project, as analysts become more familiar with the context. Consequently, it is worth performing several iterations, with the results of each iteration feeding into the questions addressed in the next.

Investigating in Context

By carefully choosing the questions to be addressed, the analyst selectively probes the user's world. Interviewees do not need to be a statistically representative sample, but they should span a wide range of opinions and needs. Some attention should be paid to ensuring a spread of ages, genders, positions within the company, workplaces, experience, degree of specialist knowledge, cultural background, etc.

Contextual inquiries take place on site and in a work situation. This way, the analyst can observe the interviewee and ask targeted questions about what they observe. The interviewee will reflect on his or her actions, thereby exposing any applied expert knowledge.

To achieve this, the analyst needs to adopt a collaborative approach. The analyst and interviewee discuss any problems relating to the work activity which has just been demonstrated, as well as the technical context and scope for improvement. The analyst collects everything discussed in the interview – forms, screenshots, sketches of relevant technical context, audio recordings of the conversation, etc.

A technique known as 'apprenticing' helps to gain deeper understanding of a task if the task can be learned in a reasonable amount of time. The interviewee instructs the analyst so that the analyst understands and is able to carry out the task – and not the other way round.

Spontaneous tasks are sometimes difficult to observe. Reconstructing situations based on artefacts is an option for such tasks, especially if these are also long running tasks. Another could be to let interview partners themselves record the task execution and conduct an interview afterwards based on the recording.

Not in all situations, work can be observed and an interview can be conducted at the same time. Where the product being developed is very new and tasks do not yet exist, the analyst can make use of draft designs, prototypes or comparable existing products. The closer the setting is to the reality of the planned application the greater the value of user responses.

Analysing the Data Collected

Analysis is carried out based on the documents, notes, sketches and video and audio recordings collected. Working in a mixed team of analysts and developers offers various benefits. Analysts and developers ask different questions and take different approaches in seeking solutions. In particular, this provides developers with the opportunity to familiarise themselves with the work environment. The team extracts the following information:

- *Objectives, needs, problems, values and characteristics of the interviewees*: In Sect. 3.2 we show how, based on this information, the team characterises the target audience using personas.
- *Tasks, processes and activities*: This information is used as a basis for describing future processes with the new system.
- *Difficulties, and users' attempts to find solutions using current tools*: This information helps the team drill down to key user needs and suitable functions to meet these needs.
- *Technical terminology and information*: When designing a new solution, a precise understanding of objects and data in the working environment is indispensible. In software development, it is usual to use a domain model to model this kind of information. Contextual inquiry provides an excellent basis for creating such a model. The team will find most of the information it requires in the various forms and documents it has collected and in existing software applications.

Figure 3.2 shows an effective way of analysing large volumes of data. The team records relevant observations and insights on cards and then holds a workshop at which the cards are interpreted, arranged and used to draw conclusions. Through a multi-stage process involving collaboration and idea-sharing between the workshop participants, the insights gained coalesce into a set of requirements to be complied

Fig. 3.2 Affinity diagrams promote active exchange of ideas between workshop participants when analysing qualitative data

with in designing the new solution. The technique is known as an affinity diagram, after the practice of grouping cards into related topics.

[Beyer et al. 98] describe an extension of this technique, **contextual design**, in which the results obtained from contextual inquiry are captured in graphic models. Graphic models are well suited for illustrating the five contextual perspectives and provide useful starting points and insights for designing a new solution. Adverse events can, for example, be investigated by using an *information flow model to* model communication between people involved in the event. Figure 3.3 shows part of a sample model.

Supplementing Business Modelling

Contextual inquiry supplements business analysis and business modelling. Business models show consolidated and standardised processes within a business. They do not, however, cover problem resolution strategies, short cuts or optimisation measures employed by a particular employee, or how that employee agrees things with colleagues. Business models say nothing about the actual physical and cultural environment in which business processes are used. Contextual inquiry aims to bridge this gap and ensure that projects take into account day-to-day operational factors.

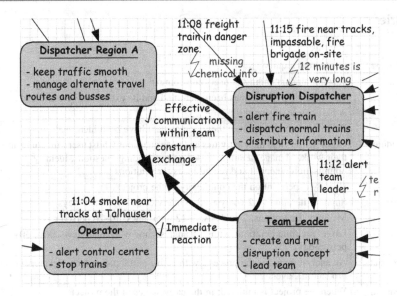

Fig. 3.3 Diagram of information flows showing communication during an adverse event. It shows the complex web of communications between those involved in full detail and flags up strengths and weaknesses

Real Life Innovation

Innovation within a business arises from a variety of sources – new and better technologies allow for new products and engender new fields of business. Optimising business processes exposes new ways forward and ensures that a company is better able to exploit its potential. Contextual inquiry opens up another new source of innovation. It exposes widespread patterns, tried and tested approaches to problem resolution and unsolved problems in the work environment – factors offering potential for really useful products which appeal directly to users.

Points to Watch

- No-one likes to be observed going about their work if it is not clear what the analysis will be used for. Achieving the required goal requires a transparent, open, interested, collaborative attitude.
- Bear in mind the questions you are looking to address when carrying out your analysis. Project teams have been known to get lost in the vast volumes of information during analysis.
- Keep a record of how you came to your conclusions. Some day, one of your clients is going to want to know why a particular feature has been included.

In Brief

Technique	Contextual inquiry
Result	A sound understanding of users and context
	Optimisation potential has been identified and its extent can be estimated
	A basis for assessing utility
	Requirements arising from the usage context have been identified
Procedure	Observe users and their activities and pose questions whilst users are going about their work. Manage iterations based on outstanding questions. Identify optimisation potential and record ideas for solutions
Work involved	Heavily dependent on the complexity of the project
	Small: 1 iteration, 1–2 analysts, 3–6 interviews: 3–8 person-days
	Medium: 2 iterations, 2 analysts, 6–12 interviews: 10–20 person-days
	Large: multiple iterations with 3–5 analysts and 6–12 interviews each: 30+ person-days
Participants	An analyst manages the process, with active participation from developers and product managers
Scheduling	When the project is initiated; in the early stages of the project

3.2   Modelling Reality: Personas and Scenarios

An insurance company is developing a software system to administer claims and payments made. The specification includes the actor 'clerk' and a major use case 'record claim'. A heated discussion ensues at one workshop, when a number of users are involved in discussing an early prototype. While one clerk finds the suggestion of presenting all required information clearly excellent, another bemoans the large number of input fields and dependencies. It turns out that the first clerk uses the existing system on a daily basis and records large numbers of claims, whilst the second clerk enters data for a small number of special cases a few times a month only, and consequently has no need of many of the available features. The prototype clearly meets the needs of the first user only, and not of the second user.

This section is concerned with personas and scenarios. These are two instruments for modelling differing user requirements and using them to derive appropriate solutions.

Personas

Personas represent archetypal users and embody those user goals, behaviours and characteristics which are relevant to the product being developed. The methodology was introduced and publicised by interaction designer Alan Cooper [Cooper

Jack

- Works on the system daily
- Handles standard cases
- Works on the phone with headset
- Uses keyboard heavily
- Hands-over complex cases to a case manager

43 years old

claims department

in insurance business for 24 years

commercial apprenticeship

« Time pressure is high. They expect less than seven minutes per case.»

« The many clicks to navigate drive me mad. Why can't I see everything I need on one screen?»

« I know the system by heart.»

« Customers should feel respected and understood.»

« You really need a thick skin to do this job.»

Fig. 3.4 Personas illustrate important user characteristics and requirements relevant to a planned new product

04]. The name has its origins in the ancient Greek theatre. A *persona* was a mask which served both to characterise the actor's role and to amplify their voice – we find it to be a very apt term. Figure 3.4 shows a sample persona.

Personas are developed based on information on the future user base for a system. This information can come from sources such as workshops with users, contextual inquiry, questionnaires, usability walkthroughs on existing systems, etc. An analyst will put together proposals which will then be validated with stakeholders, or alternatively personas may be created in joint workshops. A persona should reflect those user characteristics which are relevant to product design.

In the above example, two personas, Jack and Nick, could be used to represent the two different user groups. Jack and Nick have radically different goals and use the application in very different ways. Whilst Jack processes many cases per day and is very familiar with the current system, Nick uses the system only occasionally for individual, complex cases.

What User Characteristics Should You Be Recording

Over the course of a project, several personas, each representing a stereotypical user, will be created. A persona can provide information on the following characteristics:

- user objectives
- profession, job, responsibilities and tasks
- specialist education and training, knowledge and skills

- patterns of behaviour and ways of doing things
- values, fears, aspirations, preferences
- general computer skills
- knowledge of related products, previous systems, competing products
- areas where the current situation could be improved
- expectations for the new solution

The character created should be memorable. Their characteristics should be easy to internalise. A little extra information can help breathe life into a persona:

- name, age, gender
- pithy character traits
- image, sketch, portrait
- appropriate quotes from interviews
- a day in the life narrative

To an engineer, these kinds of characteristics, especially 'soft' characteristics such as goals, values, fears etc., may at first glance appear somewhat superfluous. Factors like these exert a powerful influence over how people behave, however.

Sharpening Up the New Solution

The project team casts an eye over the characters. One of the analysts pipes up, "Jack and Nick are very different. Aren't we going to need to create two different user interfaces?" Discussion commences. How should the project team deal with the differing personas? Are some user groups more or less important than others?

Personas can be categorised as shown in Table 3.3.

How the project team categorises Jack and Nick is a conscious choice. If they are both categorised as primary personas, the team will design two different optimised user interfaces. If, by contrast, Nick is designated as a non-persona, the interface will not be optimised for this user group.

Table 3.3 Categorising personas helps to spotlight specific user groups and thus to prioritise requirements when designing a new product

Type	Significance
Primary persona	The product is optimised and the user interface designed for their needs and requirements
Secondary persona	Their needs are largely covered by those of a primary persona. Minor additions only are required
Supplementary persona	Their needs are covered in full by a primary persona
Non-persona	A persona whose needs the project team explicitly does not take into consideration

> **Food for Thought**
> Think back to an interesting project. Were users discussed? Were certain user groups consciously or unconsciously excluded from consideration? What difference would using personas have made to the project?

Scenarios

Usage scenarios or *scenarios* are a key element in any user-centred development process. They form a bridge between requirements and the design for a new solution.

A scenario uses a realistic example to describe how a user will interact with a planned system. Using simple sentences or bullet lists, a specific process is presented from the user perspective in the usage context. As with personas, the emphasis is more on accuracy of content than formal correctness.

Figure 3.5 shows a short scenario illustrating a new insurance application. It describes in a few sentences how claims will be received in future using the new system. It reflects a range of interrelated user requirements:

- display the caller's name and details automatically
- display all current insurance policies for a customer
- rapid system response times

Scenarios are produced based on system requirements. They can be developed iteratively or in workshops in conjunction with users. A major advantage of scenarios is that they are simple to understand. They can be checked, supplemented or corrected by various parties – the client, users, the development team – at an early stage. In other words, by using scenarios, the analyst is *modelling* the requirements for a new system. A scenario exhibits the following characteristics:

Usage Scenario 1: Recording a claim

It's 3pm; Jack's phone rings. His new laptop with the big screen displays the caller's telephone number, name and other details. Jack picks up the call and greets the impatient customer, who wishes to report a broken window. As this customer has a number of insurance policies, Jack selects the relevant policy from the overview screen. He then records the details of the customer's claim.

Fig. 3.5 A scenario gives a first impression of the new solution – already in the first stages of development

- It is produced for a specific user group, takes into account their characteristics and meets their needs.
- It represents a specific example of using the system.
- It illustrates how users will use the new software in their real environment.
- It flags up points which are relevant for developing the new solution.
- It does not limit itself to the simple case where everything runs smoothly – it also describes important exceptions and errors.

Using Scenarios

Scenarios can be utilised at various points during development of a new solution and to various ends:

- *Recording and validating requirements:* Mulling over specific examples enables the client and users to visualise, scrutinise and supplement requirements. Scenarios can be viewed as initial prototypes of a new system.
- *Specification*: Scenarios illustrate product use in a real context and supplement the use case model (see Sect. 3.5). They enable developers to understand processes and context. In agile projects, scenarios are a good source for generating user stories (cf. Sect. 3.5). Scenarios introduce a specific usage into the discussion.
- *Basic user interface concept*: Design scenarios are used to describe user interface processes. This enables interaction with the interface to be modelled and, with the feedback of users, optimised. Technical requirements can be checked by developers.
- *Usability test scenarios* (see Sect, 3.7): Scenarios serve as a basis for evaluating a system or prototype in conjunction with users.
- *Test scenarios*: Scenarios can be used to generate test scenarios for testing the software.
- *Training*: Scenarios can be used to train users and as a basis for producing instructions.

Their use throughout the development process makes scenarios an extremely effective instrument in developing interactive systems. For a more in-depth examination of scenario-based development, we refer you to [Rosson et al. 02].

Background: The Power of a Good Example

Analysts take great care to use formally correct, precise formulations. A specification for a new system needs to allow very little room for interpretation. To produce formally correct formulations, it is necessary to generalise across a range of possible cases. The risk here is that reality can sometimes get left out of the equation.

The clerk records a customer's claim is a formally correct way of formulating the set of circumstances in the example in Fig. 3.5 (scenario 1). But this says little about the actual situation. In the above example, it is obvious that Jack will not be the only person using the new system. Furthermore, the system will not be used solely to record claims for broken windows. A key requirement in the above case is that the user is able to select the correct insurance policy (e.g. contents insurance) rapidly (as the customer is waiting on the other end of the phone) and accurately, based on the details provided by the customer. This requirement only becomes clear on outlining a specific usage situation and is hard to express in a formally correct, generalised description.

An example, by contrast, is neither unambiguous nor exhaustive. Interestingly, the human brain is excellent at deriving rules from examples. It is often possible to describe a set of circumstances faster, more comprehensibly and sometimes even more precisely using a few good examples than with a formal specification. Personas and scenarios take advantage of this fact. By reflecting a significant, coherent, realistic example, they are able to sketch an outline of how a planned system will be used relatively precisely early in the development process without requiring that the details be precisely defined.

The User Perspective

Personas and scenarios enable the project team to take the user's perspective and argue from the user's point of view. They are principally used for designing the system or product and optimising the user interface. A scenario could, for example, illustrate the sequence in which Jack looks for, reads and enters information. Comparing this to a similar scenario involving Nick would flag up the differences in how they use the system. This allows the right mix of supportive, restrictive and flexible features to be defined for different user groups.

Personas and scenarios also help project teams to assess competitor products and previous products. How well does someone resolve the case outlined in the scenario? This provides valuable information on the strengths and weaknesses of other solutions.

Taking the user's perspective changes the terms of the discussion. Participants are encouraged to take an alternative perspective (cf. Sect. 1.2). Discussion proceeds from the point of view of the persona, rather than from an individual perspective based on personal experience or stereotyped ideas. The result is a more objective debate. Instead of arguing over whether or not the user would understand a particular concept, it is possible to examine which persona is familiar with the concept. The more solid the data used to derive the personas, the more objective the discussion.

Points to Watch

- Ensure that misconceptions about users do not cause development work to miss the mark. Personas should be created based on knowledge about (future) users obtained from sources such as interview findings, contextual inquiry, observations and questions.
- It is not always possible to talk to users. In this case, personas provide a useful means of uncovering assumptions about users and facilitating discussion about differing viewpoints, and can contribute to achieving a shared understanding.

Where it is not possible to talk to users, it can be worthwhile evaluating information from specialists, call centres, training sessions and other secondary sources.

- Personas enable a project team to consciously focus on relevant user characteristics. In this sense, they are part of the process of scoping the project and an important means of planning user-centred activities.
- The project team should keep the number of personas to a minimum. A separate user interface or separate view will be designed around each primary persona. Multiple secondary personas indicate that the objectives of the user interface are too broadly defined or too unclear.
- In the event of changes to requirements over the course of the project, modifying and ensuring consistency of personas and scenarios can prove time-consuming. Consequently the value of personas and scenarios as tools for modelling detailed requirements is limited. Their strength is in conveying important information in a quasi-summarised form for uses such as product vision or to complement use cases.
- Personas are not a quantitative description of target groups. Personas embody those aspects of the user which are relevant to development, whereas the focus in defining target groups is on factors relevant to sales and marketing.
- Personas are not market segments. Market segmentation involves grouping potential purchasers according to intrinsic characteristics (e.g. customers aged 18–35). The characteristics of personas, by contrast, do not indicate a grouping – that is not their purpose. They reflect the needs of a single user group and focus on interaction with the future product.

In Brief

Technique	Personas and scenarios
Result	Detailed characterisation of user groups
	Identification of usage scenarios
	The team adopts a user perspective
Procedure	Compile a list of key user characteristics for a new system and use this list to develop and breathe life into personas. Develop scenarios for how users interact with the new system. Utilise personas to discuss and evaluate from the user perspective
Work involved	Modelling personas: 1–5 person days
	Developing scenarios including feedback: 3–10 person days
	Includes work for the client and the project team. This figure assumes that required and solid data are available
Participants	An analyst creates personas and scenarios. The client, analyst, software architect, developers, specialists, etc. hold discussions from the user's perspective
Scheduling	Personas are developed during scoping of the project and thereafter refined. Scenarios are primarily produced during the detailing phase in order to elaborate requirements and key aspects of the user interface

3.3   **Just Communicate: Storyboards**

Nowadays we can send a message around the world in one-seventh of a second, but it takes years to drive an idea through a quarter-inch of human skull. (Charles F. Kettering)

Software developers, clients, representatives from relevant departments and users all talk different languages. Let's take an example from an actual project – a software architect wanted representatives from the relevant departments to tell him whether optimistic or pessimistic locking was required. (Don't worry – the meaning of the two terms is not relevant to our point.) The software architect needed to decide how the new software would deal with the case where multiple users attempt to access the same data at the same time. The problem lay in his inability to formulate the question such that the departmental representatives were able to understand and answer it.

In this section we introduce **storyboards** as a means of communication between the client, users and developers. Storyboards are also used in fields such as the film industry, where they help the director convey the structure of the film to the actors and the rest of the film team. They depict factors such as perspective, lighting, facial expression, costumes, etc.

Visualising the Application

A storyboard illustrates how a system or product will be used. It depicts key aspects of system usage visually and is used to communicate between all of the various parties involved in a project. A storyboard is essentially a scenario put into visual form (cf. Sect. 3.2).

Depending on what it is intended to communicate, various options for producing a storyboard are available, ranging from sketch-like or realistic-looking user interface sequences (*user interface storyboard*), to picture stories depicting context and actors. Figure 3.6 shows an extract from a storyboard.

Analysts use storyboards where text alone is inadequate. Analysts benefit from two strengths of such a visual device:

- Images can be used to convey factors which are inexpressible or hard to express using text, such as novel concepts for which the terminology does not yet exist.
- Showing how it will be used, and by whom allows having a significant usage experience.

Storyboards are therefore useful for illustrating the following features:

- user interface dialog flows
- difficult to understand concepts or information
- important aspects of the usage context
- special or complex environments in which the system will be used

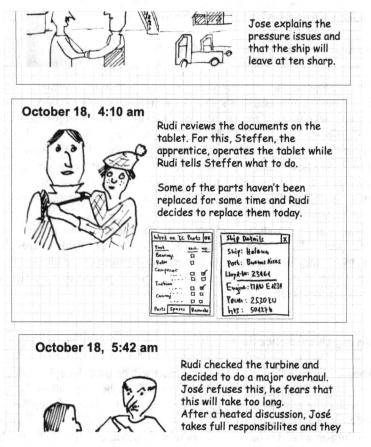

Fig. 3.6 A storyboard is used to convey an initial impression of the planned new application

Telling a Story

A storyboard tells a story about how users profitably employ a new system. The story conveys information on proposals and decisions relating to the range of features, design, software architecture, etc. The storyboard is implicitly posing the following question: "We as a project team believe that this solution meets your needs and can be implemented in this way. In what areas are we mistaken and what concerns do you have?" To allow this to happen, the following points need to be considered:

- The story should recount a specific sample case.
- It should be located in a specific place and time.
- It should explain the context and depict critical points in detail.
- The case depicted should be non-trivial.
- The characters involved should be well characterised.

- The story should plausibly explain why the characters act as they do.

A degree of realism and details of critical points can help to stimulate useful discussion and to reveal misunderstandings or discrepancies.

What Should a Storyboard Contain?

Storyboard details are firmed up over the course of a project as new information comes to light. The storyboard may start out by simply sketching out initial ideas or different options; later on it will incorporate the outcome of previous decisions. Storyboards express the following aspects of a planned system:

- needs which have and have not been taken into account
- changes to business processes
- changes in working practices
- included and explicitly excluded features
- the basic structure of the user interface
- selected details of the user interface

This list is not exhaustive. Depending on what it is intended to communicate, a storyboard will not necessarily include information on all of the above points.

Communication with a Purpose

Storyboards can be used in various situations and for various different purposes:

- to discuss an idea or proposed solution with users and other stakeholders
- to check that needs and the technical context have been correctly understood and clear up any misunderstandings
- to discuss advantages and disadvantages of various options
- to keep people informed of changes and thus (for example) promote acceptance of a new tool
- to stimulate curiosity
- to let managers know how the new solution is transforming their vision into reality
- to help developers understand relevant usage requirements and to show why certain decisions have been taken
- to provide users with an insight into the system during training events
- to market projects to clients, the management team and users

Injecting Reality into a Workshop

In a workshop, storyboards are an excellent means of conveying the reality of how a system is used. Based on the stories recounted by storyboards, participants can discuss their assumptions, reflect on how these differ from current procedures and clarify misunderstandings using real-life example.

So if the software architect in our above example wants to know how the application should respond when more than one user wants to work on the same data simultaneously, a user interface storyboard can be used as a basis for stimulating discussion with representatives from the relevant departments. They can then evaluate the consequences for their work and select the best solution. Not only will the software architect receive a properly reasoned answer to his question, he will also find out much about the intended users and their work.

In Brief

Technique	Storyboards
Result	Illustrates how the new system will be used
	Promotes client and user acceptance
	Provides feedback on ideas and decisions
	Communicates context to the project team
Procedure	Produce a visual representation of processes from the user perspective based on available information. Validate these with clients, users and members of the project team and incorporate any changes
Work involved	Approx. 1–2 person days per storyboard. This figure assumes that required and solid data are available
Participants	An analyst produces the storyboard
	The client, users, software architect and developers provide feedback
Scheduling	Early in the project for the purpose of marketing the project to sponsors
	During requirements engineering (in order to obtain feedback)
	In later phases for induction and training purposes

3.4   Scribbling for Intermediates: UI Prototyping

Engineers create prototypes in order to test out selected characteristics of a new solution – how well it works, for example, or the technology used. User-centred engineering employs user interface prototyping (**UI prototyping**) to design, evaluate and enhance aspects of the user interface prior to the creation of a functional system. Because this often involves the use of very simple tools such as paper and pencil, this is frequently referred to as **lo-fi prototyping**.

Scope of a UI Prototype

Depending on the objective, different types of UI prototype may be used. Prototypes can be characterised according to the following dimensions:

- *Functionality:* How much of the planned functionality for the user interface should the prototype demonstrate? Does this functionality represent a selected subset of features or is the intention to present the functionality in its entirety?
- *Depth of function:* With how much detail should individual features be reproduced? Should, for example, multi-stage calculations be merely hinted at or are the individual steps and the results of these steps of crucial importance?
- *Fidelity of appearance:* To what extent should the look and feel of the prototype reflect that of the final product?
- *Interactivity:* How interactive should the prototype be? Are functioning examples required in order to illustrate complex processes or are static representations of the user interface sufficient?
- *Data content:* Should real data be used or are realistic examples or even placeholders for labels and informational content sufficient? How relevant is the volume of information displayed?
- *Technical maturity:* How much of the user interface technology to be used in the final version should feature in the prototype? Does the prototype need to be developed using the development environment for the target platform or are simple drawing tools adequate?

Figure 3.7 shows different types of UI prototype with varying fidelity to the final appearance.

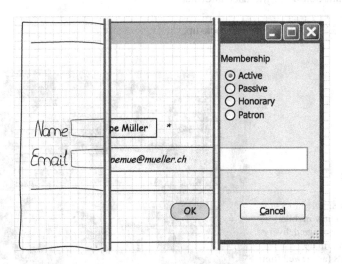

Fig. 3.7 Different types of UI prototype. *Left*: simple hand drawing. *Centre*: Wireframe. *Right*: final look and feel

All prototypes involve a compromise between the amount of work required to produce them and their purpose. Before starting work on a UI prototype, you should therefore ensure that you are clear about what questions you are trying to answer. This will enable you to select a suitable form of prototype. The following sections list some typical purposes for UI prototypes.

Clarifying Requirements

Based on information collected using contextual inquiry, the team uses paper and pencil to produce initial sketches of the user interface. Information on terminology and data is obtained from existing forms and applications. Observed processes illustrate the sequence in which users utilise this information. The initial sketches are compiled into a simulated user interface and discussed with users.

The **mock-ups** described above can be used to run through and discuss specific cases with users. This is not about system design, it is about making user requirements more tangible with the aid of simple tools, enabling the project team to identify any misunderstandings. It also enables them to identify additional user needs:

- essential information content
- functionality and processes
- integration into business processes
- data exchange with other systems and applications
- representation of tables, graphics, features, etc.
- important details of the user interface

Figure 3.8 shows a sample mock-up.

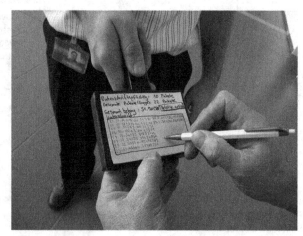

Fig. 3.8 A simple mock-up of a planned new mobile scanner for package delivery was used to firm up requirements (as viewed from the user perspective) in the early design phase

Developing a Basic User Interface Concept

One of the core tasks when designing a user interface is to develop a **basic user interface concept** which enables users to perform the tasks they need to perform. The objective is to specify the principles underlying the user interface. How does the user navigate menus and dialogs? How is information structured and displayed? Does the system need to be optimised for specific technologies (e.g. for touchscreen operation)?

The starting point is the previously elaborated personas and scenarios and the agreed requirements. Simple prototypes help the user interface designer play through scenarios and develop a suitable concept. The basic user interface concept should ultimately incorporate the following elements:

- basic structure and screen layout
- display and input devices
- information architecture and structure
- use and behaviour of windows
- key control elements
- navigation via menus, buttons and links
- input validation and display of error messages
- concepts for storage of information and states
- undo and redo
- principles of interaction, such as gestures, direct manipulation, drag & drop and pop-up menus

Consideration also needs to be given to technical aspects of the target platform, such as input and output media, operating system, screen size and resolution.

Optimising the User Interface

A poorly formulated label can be enough to prevent users from being able to use a machine correctly. A warning message which pops up and has to be dismissed repeatedly will drive frequent users to distraction. Laborious mouse operations will act as a brake on workflows.

User interface designers should therefore prototype key segments of the user interface and evaluate them with users (cf. Sect. 3.7). Below we list a few important questions to be explored:

- Does the user interface permit users to perform their work fluently?
- Are there any hurdles or stumbling blocks for people using the system for the first time?
- Is the navigation process efficient?
- Are users able to find the information they require?

- Do users notice and correctly interpret warning messages?
- Does the user interface fit in with the details of workflows?

Critical functions should be modelled using a realistic amount of real data. This enables users to run through selected cases and assess the fitness for purpose of the user interface.

Make Sure It Looks Good

Visual designers use prototypes to quickly develop different design options and to elucidate design details so to produce not only an aesthetic GUI but also one that uses an efficient visual language. When working with prototypes, it is important to find the right fit between functionality and aesthetics. User interface designers will therefore need to think about the following points:

- the arrangement of control elements
- the alignment of labels
- how elements are grouped
- colours and contrast
- font use
- style and presentation of icons
- other graphic elements

Such considerations generally necessitate a tool which allows graphic design of control elements. Many graphics programs are available which include predefined templates for the most commonly used control elements in modern user interfaces, whilst at the same time permitting fast, detailed design work.

Specifying the User Interface

A user interface prototype can be used to specify many aspects of the user interface in a clearly understandable format. Agile development teams which prefer light-weight documentation can use UI sketches to record discussion outcomes for later development work. During the specification process, a prototype can be used for the following purposes:

- to illustrate the range of features
- to demonstrate the mode of operation
- to specify user interface elements
- to demonstrate navigation and user interaction
- to provide a visual impression of the planned solution
- to estimate the development work involved in implementation

Table 3.4 Depending on the purpose it is intended to serve, different aspects are represented in the user interface prototype

Purpose	Dimension
Clarifying requirements	Substantial functionality (in multiple prototypes) with a realistic level of detail
Producing a basic user interface concept	Medium visual fidelity
	Selected functions in detail
	Partial interactivity
Optimising the user interface	High visual fidelity
	Interactive for selected functions
	Real data is often required
	Frequently requires a high level of technical maturity
Making sure it looks good	High visual fidelity
Specifying the user interface	Mid to high scope and level of functionality
	Mid to high degree of interactivity

In general, when specifying the user interface, a prototype needs to illustrate the range of functions and, at selected points, display a realistic level of functionality. A degree of interactivity is also useful as it permits visualisation of a range of user interface states. Consequently, such prototypes are often created using technology similar to that which will be used in the target solution. For simple products, graphics and image manipulation software may be sufficient.

Table 3.4 gives an overview of the intended purposes listed above and of the dimensions of the corresponding prototype.

Paper Prototyping

Sadly, we adults take the view that drawing is something best left to children and artists and fail to treat it as a serious activity. In this section, there is one thing we want to make quite clear – drawing is a necessity. Using paper and pencil to produce an initial prototype has several advantages:

- Almost everyone can do it.
- Simple sketches are quick to produce and modify.
- Less time is spent on details than with graphics software.
- No technical tools are required.
- It's possible to sketch non-standard control elements quickly.
- Several people can collaborate on a paper prototype.
- A paper prototype is easy to crumple up and discard.

For the reasons given above, activities such as requirements analysis can be carried out more efficiently with paper and pencil than with electronic tools. Paper prototypes are also excellent for visualising ideas produced in interviews and workshops.

Another important point is that the effect produced by a paper mock-up differs from that produced by an electronic prototype. Paper prototypes send out the signal that there is still ample room for change and that even low level issues remain open to discussion. Consequently, it is possible to focus more on processes and conceptual structure. The air of finality of a prototype means that people tend to assume that the broad concept is already fixed and all that remains to be clarified are a few final details. A comprehensive overview of this topic can be found in *Paper Prototyping* [Snyder 03].

An Iterative Approach

User interface prototyping is an iterative process. Boiled down to its essentials, this is illustrated in Fig. 3.9.

Here are simple step-by-step instructions for this iterative process you can start with:

- Step 1: Be clear on what you want to achieve with the iteration.
- Step 2: Identify a situation your users encounter for which the system should provide a solution and that will help you with your iteration's goals.
- Step 3: Identify the user types involved (e.g. personas) and what they really want to achieve in this situation, their goals, their values, their dreams.
- Step 4: Develop – or refine, if you already have something – a reasonable narrative on how users will behave, step-by-step, given they have the new product.
- Step 5: Develop or refine the UI prototype along this narrative.
- Step 6: Evaluate the prototype and your scenario together with users.

You may have difficulty identifying a fitting scenario, or knowing what users really want to achieve or elaborating the optimal scenario. This is a sure sign that some more research is appropriate, e.g. with contextual inquiry.

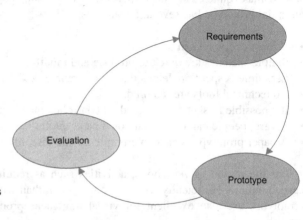

Fig. 3.9 UI prototypes are used to evaluate requirements in an iterative process

Table 3.5 Overview of various types of prototyping tools

Tool	Use
Paper and pencil, whiteboard, slides	These tools are particularly suitable for use in workshops and interviews and for exploratory sketches
Office applications *Microsoft PowerPoint, Apple Keynote*	Can be used to model basic interactivity with a minimum of effort
Image manipulation software *Adobe Photoshop*	Complete control over graphic design
Graphics programs *OmniGraffle, Microsoft Visio, Adobe Fireworks*	Provide predefined templates for standard control elements. Can thus be used to quickly produce good, genuine looking mock-ups
UI prototyping tools *Axure RP, Balsamiq Mockups, Just-in-mind Prototyper*	Specially developed for UI prototyping, these tools support the design process right from interactive sketching through to implementation on the target platform
Multimedia tools *Adobe Director, Adobe Flash*	Particularly useful for interactive prototypes with exacting design requirements and animations
Programming tools *HTML editors, development tools* *Microsoft Expression Blend, Adobe Flex*	Interactive prototypes involving large data volumes and complex behaviours

Some Common Prototyping Tools

Various tools are available for producing user interface prototypes. Table 3.5 shows some of the options available.

Figure 3.10 shows a sketch-like draft user interface produced using justinmind prototyper®. It offers some level of interactivity and can be used for UI prototyping.

Points to Watch

- User interface prototyping is an iterative activity. Don't invest too much time in perfecting it before obtaining feedback.
- It's worth choosing a tool able to produce different variants and implement changes without too much effort. There is a tendency to turn to programming tools to produce UI prototypes prematurely.

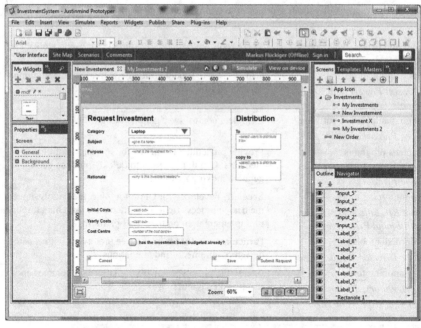

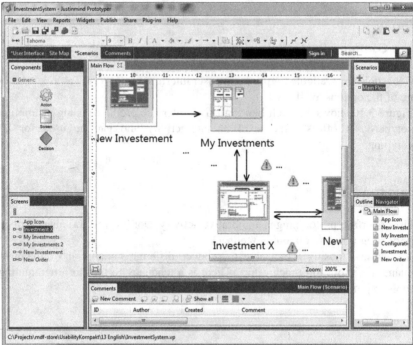

Fig. 3.10 Using a prototyping tool allows to quickly mock up an interactive prototype without programming skills

- For devices, prototypes should demonstrate the software together with the hardware. The number, size and arrangement of hardware control elements have a big effect on the basic display concept.

In Brief

Technique	User interface prototyping
Result	Evaluation of requirements
	Identify details of the user interface
	Optimise the user interface
Procedure	Production of prototypes and evaluation with users
Work involved	The work involved is heavily dependant on the purpose of the prototype. Some ball park figures for prototype production:
	– Paper: minutes or hours
	– Visio: hours or days
	– Photoshop: days or weeks
	– Development tools: days to months
Participants	An analyst to evaluate initial ideas
	A user interface designer to elaborate functionality, determine what information needs to be displayed and produce a basic user interface concept
	Developers, users and client to provide feedback
Scheduling	Early in the project, in order to firm up ideas and collect requirements
	During the specification process, in order to work out and evaluate details of the user interface

3.5 Taking It Forward into Development: Use Cases

Use cases have their origins in the software engineering field and are a widely used tool for specifying technical systems.

Given that their function is to illustrate the behaviour of a system from the user perspective, treatment of use cases in the UX literature is surprisingly spartan. The processes a user will run through on a system are largely determined by the use cases which get specified. It therefore follows that use case design exerts a significant influence on the user's experience with the planned system. For the reasons given above we have decided to include them in our collection of the most important user-centred techniques. We will, however, limit ourselves to a brief summary and a description of their relationship to other techniques.

The Use Case Model

Use cases describe a system's (planned) functionality and thus how it will interact with the outside world. A major strength of use cases is that they break the diversity of system functionality down into (from the user's perspective) coherent units and gradually define this functionality more precisely. A further benefit of use cases is that they use natural language which remains comprehensible to everyone involved in a project throughout the development process.

To describe a specific feature, the project team uses **actors**, which interact with the system. Actors embody roles performed by users or other systems. A use case describes a functional procedure involving the system from an actor's perspective. In the case of an online book ordering application, for example, the customer who orders the book would be an actor, the process of ordering a book a use case, tracing the order another use case, rating a book a third use case, and so on. From the actor's perspective, use cases should always encompass a closed set of actions.

The use case model is used to model system functionality as part of the requirements analysis process. The system itself is treated as a black box, i.e. there is no description of how the described behaviour comes about. Individual interactions for each use case are then described and used to produce a specification for development use. Use cases thus embody the functional behaviour of a system. A use case model can also be depicted in graphic form in the form of a *use case diagram*, which provides an overview of the system's functionality and its external interfaces. Figure 3.11 shows a sample use case diagram based on UML notation.

Where Do the Actors Come From?

Actors and use cases are usually elucidated in *use case workshops* involving the client, relevant departments and users. The difficulty here is that actors do not represent actual users, but rather roles which interact with the system. A common error is to construct actors which are so over-generalised that they no longer reflect reality. This can result in important needs being overlooked or requirements from different user groups being conflated into a single actor. The result is use cases which cover a mixture of functions which would be better dealt with separately. This in turn leads to procedures which prove to be unsuitable for actual users.

A sound use case model is produced based on analysis of actual users and context. To achieve this, contextual inquiry, interviews or comparable techniques for recording user responsibilities and activities are essential.

The Use Case Specification

A use case specification describes step by step the interaction between an actor and the system. As well as the simple case where all goes according to plan, the project team also needs to consider alternative processes and error cases.

Fig. 3.11 A use case
diagram provides a useful
summary of the functionality
of a planned new application

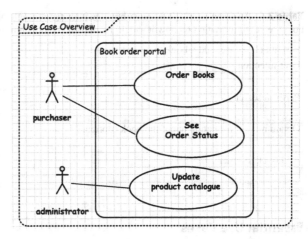

In formulating a use case, technical details should be omitted. A common mistake is to produce a use case specification which assumes certain details of the user interface. This is a bad idea for two reasons. Firstly, the described process may be able to be better implemented using an alternative interaction concept. Secondly, excessive detail can make maintaining and modifying use cases in the event of changes more difficult. A much better option is to complement the use case specification with a user interface prototype or storyboard which illustrates processes using the specific user interface. The project team can use this prototype to verify and refine the design with the client and users. In addition to natural language descriptions, flow charts can also be used to depict individual steps.

The specification does, after all, need to be comprehensible to two very different parties – the client and the development team. Use cases should therefore be both formally correct and comprehensible. [Cockburn 00] is an excellent aid for formulating good, comprehensible use cases.

Background: Functional and Non-functional Requirements

In requirements management, a distinction is made between functional and non-functional requirements.

As the name suggests, *functional requirements* deal with factors relating to the functionality of the planned system. Our book ordering system, for example, might offer search, order and rating functions. Details of functional procedures required to order a book can be firmed up using use cases.

Non-functional requirements encompass any external required conditions. In our book ordering system example, the system would have to meet certain requirements in terms of availability, response times, reliability, etc. Non-functional requirements also exert a significant effect on system usability and have a bearing on which technologies and software architectures are used. Non-functional usability criteria can also be specified in terms such as the required efficiency for users. In our example, 90 % of users should be able to search for and order a particular book in less than five minutes.

Table 3.6 An essential use case shows how the intended user interaction should unfold, but does not give any information on how it should be implemented technically

Essential use case: add a book to an order	
User intention	System responsibility
	Present a search dialog
Perform search	
	Present appropriate books
Obtain more information about the book (optional)	
	Present details of the book
Add book to order	
	Confirm

Essential Use Cases

The idea that technical details should be largely excluded from use cases has led to the concept of **essential use cases** [Constantine et al. 99]. The aim here is to describe use cases solely in terms of interaction with the system and to entirely exclude details of the technical implementation. The idea is to avoid homing in on a (potentially suboptimal) technical solution too early. The example in Table 3.6 shows a simple essential use case for a book ordering system.

User Stories

In the agile world (cf. Sect. 2.1, "Background: Agile Software Development"), user stories have been adopted in place of use cases. At first glance, the two techniques look very similar. Like a use case, a user story describes a function from the user's perspective. The title of a use case involving the actor 'customer' might be 'Ordering books', for example. A user story in the same context might be called 'As an authenticated user, I am able to place a book in the shopping basket so that I can order it afterwards'.

The differences between the two techniques are derived from the purposes for which they are used. Use cases are used to agree and specify the behaviour of the planned system and to produce requirements on the basis of which the system will be developed and tested. There are usually set templates for documenting use cases.

User stories record the intention to communicate. At an appropriate stage of the project, the user story should be discussed in detail and agreed with the right people. It should be clear to all participants what is being implemented for what purpose and how it will be tested and accepted. User stories can be fairly coarse-grained to begin with. They will be broken down and refined over the course of the project. The goal is that multiple user stories should be able to be fully implemented in a single iteration. User stories require direct, rapid communication between participants. The team therefore captures details in the form of keywords, sketches of the user interface, simple scenarios, etc. Agile teams also use personas when formulating user stories, thus creating a bridge between user requirements and development. A comprehensive introduction to user stories can be found in [Cohn 04].

Use Cases or Scenarios?

Conceptually, actors and use cases are related to personas and scenarios (see Sect. 3.2). Both are techniques used by analysts to model interaction with the system. There are, however, some important differences:

- Actors define roles which interact with the system. Personas by contrast encapsulate archetypal users and focus on the characteristics of different user groups.
- Use cases record a specific component of the system's behaviour for the development team. They make generalisations about the various usage options. By contrast, scenarios describe specific examples of system usage and illustrate usage in the actual context.

Table 3.7 clarifies these differing objectives.

In practice the two techniques are highly complementary. Realistic personas and scenarios derived from user analysis form an excellent basis for use cases. Over the course of the project, the analyst will flesh out and round off use cases to specify the entire functional behaviour of the system, including integration with external systems.

Food for Thought
Imagine a system for ordering books. Think about the actors 'customer' and the use case 'ordering a book'. Now imagine Ruth. She works at an academic library and one Monday uses this ordering system to order 219 newly published books. How does the ordering system in this case differ from the ordering system used by Lara to order the latest novel by her favourite author?

Table 3.7 Comparison of personas and scenarios with actors and use cases

Technique	Format	Objective
Actor	Role description	To group related functional procedures
Persona	Archetypal user	To characterise different user groups
Use case	Description of system behaviour	To provide a specification of functional behaviour for the development team
Scenario	Specific example of system usage	To describe usage in the actual context

An analyst writing a specification for a new system will examine various individual situations and generalise from his findings to produce an abstract model. Someone reading the specification who only has access to this abstract model will, however, be unable to work back to these specific individual cases or understand how they differ, since this information is not contained within the abstraction. Examples, on the other hand, are excellent instruments for illustrating context and procedures (cf. Sect. 3.2 "Background: The Power of a Good Example").

Checklist for Using Use Cases

- Are the actors created discernable in reality? Have they been created based on analysis of users and context? Has consideration been given to different user groups?
- From the user perspective, do the use cases encompass closed sequences of actions? Do they correspond to the identified scenarios and users' actual work processes?
- Does the use case specification take into account alternative workflows and system behaviour in the event of an error? In a user-centred system design process, these factors also need to be considered.
- Do the use cases and alternative workflows include details of their duration and frequency of occurrence?
- Do their descriptions omit technical details which would be better modelled in a user interface concept, storyboard or prototype?
- Is it clear what information the user requires to perform the intended task for each step in a use case?

In Brief

Technique	Use cases
Result	Overview of system functionality
	Detailed description of system behaviour from the user perspective
Procedure	Identify actors and use cases
	Create a use case model
	Specify use cases
	Review with stakeholders
Work involved	Designing and reviewing a use case model: 3–10 person days (including stakeholders)
	Specification (heavily dependent on the scope of system functionality): 10–15 use cases: 15–30 person days
Participants	Client, analyst, developers
Scheduling	As part of requirements analysis, following contextual inquiry or once personas and scenarios have been specified

3.6   Guidelines and Style Guides

It's like a jungle sometimes
It makes me wonder how I keep from goin' under (Grandmaster Flash, 1982)

Aren't there, maybe, some guidelines for user interfaces to help us make a better product? Indeed there are. Going by the number of hits you get when you Google 'interface guidelines', there are about 250,000. So all you need to do is follow all the relevant rules – just like a writer does when writing a book or an architect does when designing a house. That sound OK?

Different Types of Guidelines

Usability guidelines contain rules for designing user interfaces. There are a large number of reference works which fall into this category, ranging from general guidelines to detailed sets of rules and regulations.

Guidelines for user interfaces can be categorised according to their intended purpose. The list below is intended to help you understand how different user interface-related rules and regulations fit within the overall picture:

- *Legal stipulations:* Regulations, principally aimed at ensuring the safety of workers when dealing with technical devices (especially devices with monitors). It may come as some surprise to learn that some aspects of usability are legally regulated, but demonstrable disregard for these regulations can have unpleasant consequences for an employer. Within the EU, the relevant legislation is directive 90/270/EEC [EEC 90], which includes minimum requirements for human-machine interfaces.
- *Standards:* National and international standards which aim to standardise the use of technology and make using technology simpler for users by setting out design rules. The best known example is international standard ISO 9241, which defines "Ergonomics of human-system interaction" [ISO 10]. The seven criteria for a user friendly dialog system listed in Table 3.8 are widely applied (ISO/DIS 9241, part 110).
- *Collections of rules*: Collections of rules for optimising development of user interfaces. They are usually freely available. These include general **usability principles**, such as Nielsen's *Usability Heuristics* [Nielsen 93] and *Google User Experience Principles* [Google 14], as well as specific rules for certain fields. There are, for example, 'dos and don'ts' for mobile applications and 'golden rules' for good web design. Various collections are available in book form, e.g. [Johnson 07].
- *User interface patterns*: An attempt to describe recurring or similar design problems and to offer proven approaches to their resolution by using patterns. A number of helpful pattern collections for the GUI field are now available, e.g. [Tidwell 11], [Scott et al. 09]. The patterns described generally relate to a

Table 3.8 Principles of dialog design (ISO 9241-110)

Suitability for the task	The system helps the user perform tasks and supports their work processes
Self descriptiveness	The system includes explanations and is sufficiently easy to understand
Controllability	The user is able to control the dialog sequence
Conformity with user expectations	User expectations, characteristics and habits are supported
Error tolerance	Correction of errors requires no or little effort
Suitability for individualisation	The system can be customised to meet individual needs
Suitability for learning	Learning to use the system requires little effort and the system helps the user learn new functions

specific GUI technology. In practice, the boundary between pattern and element collections, the latter frequently found in style guides, is somewhat fuzzy.

- *Vendor or platform style guides:* These describe the prescribed look and feel of an application for a specific operating system. The objective is to ensure that all UI elements – input fields, list boxes, buttons, etc. – are used consistently. Good examples include *Apple Human Interface Guidelines* [Apple 92–13, Apple 08–14] and *Microsoft Windows User Experience Interaction Guidelines* [Microsoft 05–14].
- *Corporate style guides*: Rules pertaining to look and feel and corporate design with which a company's various applications are expected to comply. A distinction should be drawn between guidelines for the internal corporate application ecosystem and guidelines for applications and products for external customers. The use of corporate style guides will be described in more detail in Sect. 5.3.
- *Project style guides*: Guidelines for ensuring the consistency of the user interface during development of an application (e.g. when using several UI designers) or consumer product. In some cases, new control elements will need to be defined and described (e.g. for novel products).

Figure 3.12 shows an example from a style guide. A sortable table is used to enable users to select from longer lists. This GUI element looks the same and behaves consistently in every application. The font and contrast have been optimised for on-screen legibility and the sort function is intuitive. The colour scheme corresponds to the company's corporate design and there are no technical barriers to implementation.

Using Guidelines

First things first: even if you follow all the relevant rules, it is still possible to design a solution which, from the user perspective, is unusable. It is increasingly accepted that target groups and usage context are crucial to the actual quality of a user interface.

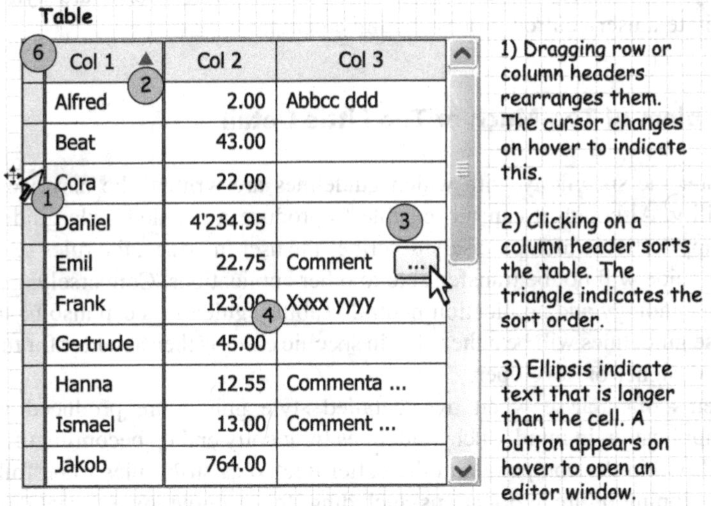

Table

Col 1	Col 2	Col 3
Alfred	2.00	Abbcc ddd
Beat	43.00	
Cora	22.00	
Daniel	4'234.95	
Emil	22.75	Comment
Frank	123.00	Xxxx yyyy
Gertrude	45.00	
Hanna	12.55	Commenta ...
Ismael	13.00	Comment ...
Jakob	764.00	

1) Dragging row or column headers rearranges them. The cursor changes on hover to indicate this.

2) Clicking on a column header sorts the table. The triangle indicates the sort order.

3) Ellipsis indicate text that is longer than the cell. A button appears on hover to open an editor window.

Fig. 3.12 Style guides define and describe user interface elements to be used when developing a new application

The principal role of user interface guidelines is as an aid to uniform, rules-compliant user interface design. Conforming to guidelines makes it easier for users to use the user interface, since it ensures that they encounter familiar elements which always behave consistently. Deciding whether a set of rules or a specific stipulation is indeed relevant for a particular application or technology does, however, require a degree of expertise. Without this expertise, blind rule-following can quickly become burdensome and ultimately even act as an obstacle to a user interface that meets the user's needs.

It is not enough to employ existing collections of rules – they are likely to be poorly applicable to your specific situation. A style guide which defines and describes the UI elements used in a large project acts as an instrument for ensuring that the system operates in a uniform manner from the user point of view. A style guide sets out a basic framework for user interface design early in the project. There is a big difference, for example, between using highly efficient controls to aid expert users or simple, self-explanatory control elements for occasional users.

A well designed style guide where visual and technical factors are in perfect harmony is extremely useful for developers. Rather than reinventing the wheel, they can re-use previously developed elements which meet ergonomic, aesthetic, corporate design and technical feasibility requirements.

Using a style guide in a large project or corporation also has an organisational function. Having user interface elements to which a name has been assigned, for which a description exists and which are familiar to all participants in a project enables user interface requirements and technical restrictions to be addressed earlier in the project. Section 5.3 looks in more detail at how using a corporate style guide can facilitate a user-centred process within a company.

The Problem of Too Much or Too Little Detail

The greater the specificity with which guidelines are written, the narrower their applicability. Although it can be sensible to produce a detailed style guide for a specific application which precisely describes the user interface, the rules set out in this style guide will not be transferrable to other applications. Conversely, general, broadly technology and application-neutral usability guidelines can also be useful. How these guidelines will be adhered to in specific cases is then a matter for the user interface designer or developer.

Problems often arise when over-detailed style guides are produced with a specific application in mind. Such guidelines frequently end up becoming officially enshrined within the company and thereafter treated as strict rules to be followed when developing future applications, including, for example, by external development teams. The result is that a development team may find itself having to adhere to rules which make no sense or may even be counterproductive in the case at hand. Serious consideration should therefore be given to the level of detail which should be aspired to in a specific case. A diagram of a sample user dialog with an explanation may be more effective than a set of narrowly formulated rules. Examples can also be easier to extrapolate to other situations.

What Should Be Specified in a Good Style Guide?

If you need to produce your own style guide or to subcontract production of a style guide to a third party, it is helpful to know what information it should contain:

- *Technical framework* and *target group*: What system does the style guide pertain to? Who will be given a copy of the guide?
- *Software ergonomics:* Generally applicable rules which should be taken into consideration in specific cases (e.g. the number of menu options) and rules pertaining to specific target groups and areas of application (e.g. dialogs which can be controlled using just the keyboard).
- *Basic structure:* Rules for the structure of an application, e.g. title bar, ribbons, navigation panel, working and help panels, status bar and dialog types.
- *Display devices and layout*: A definition of how the interface should be structured depending on screen size and resolution.
- *Input devices:* What input devices – keyboard, touch, pen, gestures, mouse, etc. – will be used and for what purpose.
- *Usage rules:* What UI elements will be used in what situation. This applies to basic operating system elements (e.g. when will radio buttons/list boxes be used), composite elements (e.g. sortable tables, wizards) and in particular to newly defined elements (e.g. a pop-up calendar for date selection).

- *Behaviour of UI elements:* Description of system response (e.g. selection of an entry, deactivation of controls).
- *Navigation:* Description of navigation elements (e.g. use of menus, links, buttons).
- *Visual design:* Colour scheme, contrasts, fonts, layout, spacing, icons, etc. Corporate design will also play a part here.
- *Technical feasibility:* Information on the technical implementation, e.g. reference to available UI components.
- *Terminology:* User interface terms and designations, how the user will be addressed, what specialist terminology will be used, how error messages are to be formulated.
- *Keyboard operation:* Shortcuts, commands, tab sequence, default buttons in dialogs.

Checklist for Employing a Style Guide

- Do specific standards or legal regulations for user interface design have to be adhered to for your application?
- Are there any existing reference works available to assist you (e.g. collections of rules or proprietary style guides)?
- Is it worth developing a style guide specifically for the project?
- Do the guidelines used have an appropriate level of detail?
- Does the style guide include items which would be better dealt with in the specification?
- Could using an integrated style guide facilitate communication within the project or company?

In Brief

Technique	Guidelines and style guides
Result	Rules-compliant user interface design
	System operates in a uniform manner
	User interface requirements are addressed
	Help for user interface developers
Procedure	Use existing collections of rules or develop a project style guide
Work involved	Depends on size and level of detail
	Collection of relevant usability guidelines: 1–2 person days
	Development of a complete project style guide: not less than 10 person days
	Corporate style guide: not less than 100 person days
Participants	Analyst, user interface designer
Scheduling	Developed in conjunction with a basic user interface concept and refined during realisation

3.7   Usability Testing

You are probably familiar with the idea of testing software and products in a *usability lab*. You may even have had the opportunity to attend *usability testing* as a spectator or participant. Although usability labs have been around for a good 30 years, they still have a relatively low profile, with few people aware of how such testing is carried out. We will therefore outline the typical procedure for formal usability testing, followed by a brief section exploring other, less formal methods.

Formal Usability Testing

Firstly, the client and test supervisor need to clarify the objective to be achieved with usability testing. Specialists make a distinction between *formative* evaluation, aimed at improving the tested system, and *summative* evaluation for quality control purposes.

As preparation for usability testing, the test supervisor and client will compile a set of tasks which the participants will undertake using the application. To achieve a degree of comparability, these tasks are the same for each participant (*standard tasks*). The quality of the results of usability testing is in large part dependent on how these tasks are prepared. In Chap. 1 we discussed the idea that the quality of a new solution depends on how well it supports user tasks and processes. Great care should therefore be taken in preparing relevant and (from the user's point of view) realistic tasks. If usage scenarios have been developed, they can be used as a basis for elaborating these tasks (see Sect. 3.2). A good test supervisor will ensure that standard tasks meet the following criteria (which you, as the person commissioning the tests, should check):

- The task should represent a realistic scenario from the user's point of view and should actually occur as described.
- The task should be formulated in terms of the user's objective in using the system, with no technical instructions on how to achieve that objective. For example, 'Find a suitable colour for a summer dress for your little girl', is more appropriate than 'Set the filter criteria to yellow and pink.'
- For the participants, the degree of difficulty involved in performing the task should be moderate. It should be soluble but not too trivial.
- Terms and labels used in the application should be avoided. For example, 'Transfer an amount of …' is more neutral than 'Select Payments' from the menu.'

As well as test tasks, the test system or prototype also needs to be prepared for the planned usage scenario. In order to present participants with a functioning system which is as realistic as possible it can be necessary to implement specific system states or tasks.

Where possible, participants should be drawn from the intended user group for the application, i.e. should be people who will or may actually use the system. Whilst for a consumer product or web application, this could be a secretary or a member of staff from a neighbouring office, for specialist applications, recruiting appropriate specialists is essential.

The number of participants required depends largely on the test objectives. In general, five to seven users are sufficient for testing the main application scenarios and instituting specific improvements using a prototype. If, on the other hand, the intention is to attain a high level of confidence that you have removed all stumbling blocks to the release of an application, further test series will be required. More on this can be found in the section 'How many test participants are required?' later in this chapter.

In some cases – a highly efficient application intended for use by expert users following an induction period, for example – it may be helpful for the participants to receive brief training in or an introduction to the application. By contrast, in the case of occasional users for, say a consumer product, it goes without saying that no prior explanation should be given.

The test supervisor should instruct each participant in the objectives and procedure of the usability test and agree a set of rules.

- The participant can pause or stop the test at any time.
- The participant is usually asked to think out loud, i.e. to comment on what they are doing for the benefit of observers.
- If the participant is unable to proceed further with a task, they can independently move on to the next task.
- Observers should intervene only where absolutely necessary. They should avoid influencing the progress of the tests as far as possible. Conversations with the user should be conducted under controlled conditions, e.g. via an intercom.

During the actual test session, the participants work in a dedicated test room and use the test application to perform the set tasks. Figure 3.13 shows the layout of a typical usability lab.

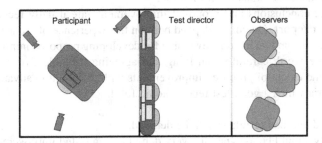

Fig. 3.13 Schematic representation showing the major components of a usability lab. Users use the new product to perform tasks in the test room. Observers record any deficits. Interaction with the user interface is recorded on video for later analysis

Fig. 3.14 UI prototypes can be used during usability testing to allow early identification of user requirements as well as usability issues and improve the user interface

Observers should include client representatives, developers and usability experts. The test supervisor and observers are often separated by a pane of glass from the test room, in order not to disturb or influence the user. The screen or product for testing, and often additionally the user's face and the situation as a whole, are video recorded. Figure 3.14 shows such a view (see also Fig. 2.10 in Sect. 2.2 for an example video recording).

Observers record unclear or problem situations and any errors arising during application use. The test should not last longer than an hour.

After the test, the observers then analyse relevant video segments in conjunction with the participant. Initial ideas for improvements will also be discussed. The participant should have the opportunity to comment on his or her experience, either through a brief interview or in a free-form statement. It is often informal situations which yield the most valuable information.

Problems, conclusions and proposed improvements are usually recorded in a **usability test report**. Outcomes depend both on the experience of the test supervisor and observers and on the time available for developing proposed improvements. It is therefore worth carefully clarifying and agreeing the objective of usability testing and the extent of proposed improvements with the client in advance. There are set criteria which a good test report should fulfil:

- Both good and bad results should be detailed.
- A severity should be assigned to every deficit or suggested improvement.

- Deficits should be illustrated with screenshots.
- The report should include the standard tasks and a description of the participants.
- Observed problems should be clearly distinguished from personal opinions and suggestions.

The American National Standards Institute (ANSI) developed a Common Industry Format (CIF) for usability test reports which has become an international standard in 2006 [ISO 06]. Although the format of the CIF was originally designed only for summative reporting, it can be a good starting point for setting up your own report.

More information about usability testing can be found in the *Handbook of Usability Testing* [Rubin et al. 08].

Strengths and Weaknesses of Usability Testing

For a long time, formal usability testing was considered the gold standard technique for usability evaluation, and it does indeed have some major strengths:

- Laboratory conditions enable deficits in the user interface to be unambiguously demonstrated.
- Methodological quality criteria such as objectivity, reproducibility and validity are broadly met (see also "Background: Methodological quality criteria" later in this chapter).
- A usability lab offers optimal conditions for performing observations. Observers are able to get a good picture of the strengths and weaknesses of a new solution.
- Observers are forced to watch the user without becoming involved. As any usability test supervisor will tell you, the window between the test and observation rooms is principally there to stop observers from helping the user.
- Difficulties in using the new product quickly become apparent.
- The method is highly transparent to all involved. The importance of user-centred engineering is made clearly visible.

The technique does, however, have the following weaknesses:

- It tends to be used at a relatively late stage. Prototypes need to be sufficiently advanced to allow participants to work with them autonomously.
- Performing formal usability test series is laborious. Adequate time needs to be invested in developing tasks, preparing the test system, recruiting participants, performing test series in a usability lab, elaborating suggested improvements and producing test reports.
- There is a risk that test reports containing useful results will disappear into a drawer in the client's office, due either to a lack of knowledge or funds for implementing improvements. It is therefore essential that the test supervisor, client and developers sit down and discuss and prioritise deficits together. In

some instances it may even make sense to dispense with a detailed report and instead invest the time in proposing solutions.

Background: Methodological Quality Criteria

Test theory uses a number of quality criteria as a basis for determining the quality of a measurement tool used in a specific test. Knowledge of these quality criteria can be relevant when using user-centred techniques, especially when evaluating systems. The main quality criteria are:

- *Objectivity:* The results of a test should be independent of the conditions under which it is carried out. A key factor here is the independence of the people conducting the tests.
- *Reproducibility:* A test instrument should produce the same results when testing is repeated under the same conditions.
- *Validity:* The instrument should measure what it claims to measure. In our case, this means the usability of a system, and nothing else. This can in part be achieved by excluding unwanted influences (*internal validity*). Also important is the degree to which results can be generalised (*external validity*). This can be improved by increasing the number of people surveyed and by using other evaluation techniques.

Alternatives to Formal Usability Testing

A usability walkthrough is one alternative to formal usability testing. Rather than a test administrator working independently under controlled conditions in a separate test room, the test supervisor assists the user and walks them through the test. As with formal testing, the user performs realistic tasks on the test system, but the supervisor is able to intervene, ask questions and run through specific processes with the user. This can be performed in a usability lab, but can also take place elsewhere. This technique is particularly suitable for evaluating unfinished prototypes at an early stage of the process without requiring a functioning system. That the test supervisor is no longer independent under this schema and needs to know exactly how to instruct the user without exerting too great a degree of influence is self-evident.

A **mobile usability lab** is a mobile structure for conducting usability tests on site rather than in a laboratory. Rather than video recording the user interface, many test supervisors now use special software which allows user interactions to be recorded directly on the test computer. Equipped with a laptop and a webcam, this enables usability testing to be conducted without incurring the costs associated with a usability lab. Utility and outcomes are heavily dependent on the experience of the test supervisor.

Mobile usability testing is particularly appropriate where testing is to be conducted on site, for example in specialised workplaces or where the environment exerts a significant influence (say a public terminal such as a station ticket machine or open air ATM). The technical term for this is *usability field testing*.

How Many Test Participants Are Required?

Imagine you're a shop owner. You've just watched an old lady trip over the door sill at the entrance to your shop. A little later, a young man does the same. Would you replace the sill or would you wait for more people to trip over it?

Critical usability issues identified during usability testing can be just as unambiguous as the above example. If two or three participants report difficulties at the same point, it is clear that this point represents a stumbling block which needs to be dealt with. Watching a fourth or fifth user stumble at the same point is quite simply unnecessary. In other words, qualitative observations from usability testing can be used to make improvements to the user interface. Quantitative testing using large numbers of users is unnecessary (see also Sect. 3.8, "Background: Quantitative and Qualitative Methods"). Nonetheless, how many participants are required to ensure that all critical issues are identified is an important question. Below we offer some ballpark figures:

- Iterative prototyping, improving and adapting the system to better meet user needs, qualitative statements: 4–6 users per iteration. Systems with high usability requirements: 7–15 users. Risk mitigation for critical systems: no fewer than 15 participants.
- Quality control prior to launching a new system, quantitative statements: no fewer than 10 users (depending on the scale of the system and usability requirements).

In Brief

Technique	Usability testing
Result	Usability of user interface is tested
	Deficits are identified, recorded and prioritised
	Improvement measures are identified
Procedure	Testing with users using standard tasks
Work involved	Formal lab-based usability testing with 5–7 users (preparing, conducting and analysing tests): test supervisor 10 person days, client 5–10 person days, test participants 3–5 person days in total
	Usability walkthrough with 5–7 users: test supervisor 5 person days, client 3–5 person days, test participants 2–3 person days in total
Participants	Client, developers, users, test supervisor, observers
Scheduling	After producing the first prototype
	At the end of each iteration
	Prior to launch

3.8   Numerical Data: Questionnaires

Do you subscribe to the latest papers by well-known analysts and market research organisations? The figures used to produce these papers are frequently obtained using questionnaires. The methodology for producing and using questionnaires has its roots in the social sciences, in cases where personal data amenable to statistical analysis is needed for purposes such as determining attitudes, opinions and experiences, or where results need to be compared with a larger whole, as in psychological studies.

User surveys involving questionnaires are a technique for obtaining responses from large numbers of people. If you've ever put together a questionnaire to, say, survey the opinions of your co-workers or customers, you'll know that this is no simple matter. The reliability of the conclusions drawn depends on the quality of the questionnaire, the choice of respondents and on the survey being performed correctly.

Applying User Surveys

Do you recall the user-centred engineering subtasks presented in Sect. 2.2? User surveys serve two purposes – they are used to analyse users and context and they are used to evaluate the fit between a product and its users. User surveys complement the user-centred techniques presented above. In contrast to contextual inquiry and usability testing, they enable analysts to survey large numbers of people. Questionnaires allow analysts to capture and count responses.

Depending on the survey objectives and the questions which the questionnaire is designed to address, a range of instruments can be used. The spectrum ranges from simple, home-made questionnaires to standard questionnaires employing proven methodologies.

Various types of survey are used. A questionnaire may, for example, be conducted by post, be taken online or be conducted over the phone.

Questionnaires are often used with the aim of obtaining information which is representative of the user group as a whole. Because such investigations aim to obtain quantifiable figures, experts use the term *quantitative* studies (cf. *qualitative* studies). There are a range of methodological issues which need to be considered when performing quantitative studies. As this is somewhat laborious, close scrutiny should be given to the question of whether a quantitative survey is the appropriate instrument for addressing the questions you are aiming to address.

Background: Quantitative and Qualitative Methods
Empirical research distinguishes between two basic approaches to obtaining information:

* *Quantitative* studies are aimed at describing numerical properties with as much precision as possible. This usually involves surveying a representative sample and extrapolating the data collected to the population as a whole. In general, a hypothesis to be tested based on the

results is specified beforehand. In order to ensure that respondents are answering under more or less identical conditions, quantitative methods usually follow highly standardised procedures.

- *Qualitative* investigations are aimed at identifying background information, context and causal factors. Value is attached to subjective statements made by respondents. Such techniques are more flexible, open and explorative than quantitative methods. New hypotheses will often be generated in the course of such studies and pursued in a subsequent iteration. Qualitative data cannot be used to determine quantitative values.

Table 3.9 compares these two approaches.

It is important to avoid the view that a questionnaire is just a bunch of questions that gets bunged in the post to respondents. Conducting a survey requires that the person compiling the questionnaire gives careful consideration to what questions are to be answered, how the study will be conducted and how the questionnaire needs to be structured to achieve this. Methodologists use the terms *study design* and *questionnaire construction*.

Planning a User Survey

There are a number of key points to be considered in choosing a suitable **study design**:

- What questions should it answer, what hypotheses should it test? Is the aim simply to collect facts, to evaluate a system or to perform a comparison?
- How will the study be scheduled? Will data collection be a one-off process, will results from different groups be compared or will the same users be surveyed at intervals?
- How will the survey sample be selected? Randomly or according to set criteria?

Table 3.9 Comparison between *quantitative* and *qualitative* research techniques

Quantitative research	Qualitative research
Many participants	Few participants
Representative sample	Typical representatives
Testing hypotheses	Forming hypotheses
Standardised	Flexible, explorative
Countable facts	Background, context
Closed questions	Open questions
Statistical analysis	Content analysis
Simple to analyse	Complex to analyse
Examples: statistic surveys, standardised telephone interviews	Examples: contextual inquiry, stakeholder interviews, focus groups

- How many people need to be included in the survey in order to be able to draw statistically sound conclusions?
- What instruments will be used to perform the study? Will an existing questionnaire be used or will the questionnaire be produced in-house?

Questionnaire Construction

If meaningful results are to be obtained, a proper methodology needs to be used when designing and deploying a questionnaire. This is equally applicable in the case of simple questionnaires comprising a small number of questions. Before you start thinking about producing your own questionnaire, you should therefore check to see whether a standard questionnaire designed to answer the questions you want answered is already available. To design questionnaires capable of producing statistically sound conclusions, it is worth bringing in a questionnaire expert.

The following methodological factors need to be considered both when designing your own questionnaire and when selecting a standard questionnaire:

- Should it use open or closed questions? Open questions allow users to formulate their responses freely, closed questions involve selecting from set answers. Open questions can be used to illuminate all aspects of a question, but are more complicated to analyse than closed questions. Open questions are therefore better suited to qualitative studies, closed questions preferred for quantitative studies.
- Will scales (e.g. a value from 1 to 7) be used? What do these scales mean (e.g. understood – not understood, score of 1–6)? This is important when it comes to analysing and interpreting the collected data.
- How will respondents be told how to fill in the questionnaire? Will they understand the instructions?
- Will all questions be comprehensible to the target group? A questionnaire should always be tested on sample respondents.
- How much time is required to fill in the questionnaire? The longer the questionnaire, the greater the number of uncompleted questionnaires and the poorer the quality of the answers. This effect is even more pronounced in the case of online surveys than for written questionnaires.

If you want more information on the methodology involved in conducting questionnaire-based studies, we suggest you consult the relevant literature (e.g. [Robson 11]).

Analysing Users and Context

Questionnaires can be used to analyse users and usage context and can thus help to clarify requirements for a new solution. Since **requirements analysis** is largely concerned with sounding out a new field, recording details of day-to-day work and exploring causalities and context, it tends to be the domain of qualitative techniques. It can sometimes be expedient to supplement contextual inquiry, interviews and observations by clarifying certain issues or corroborating conclusions with the aid of a large pool of users. One approach might be to start out with open questions to sound out user preferences and problems with existing systems and to collect some initial ideas for improvements, then to evaluate these using a scoring system.

Questionnaires can also be used to collect specific information about users and usage which is relevant to the requirements for a new solution:

- user age, gender, education and experience
- roles, tasks and activities
- frequency with which, where and when the solution would be used
- current technical set-up, e.g. devices, operating systems, screen size and resolution, browser versions, existing applications, etc.

Market surveys for new products sometimes use this approach to try to obtain information from future users about desired functionality and the need for specific features. There are, however, limits to what can be achieved using such surveys. If, for example, respondents are not really able to picture what the new solution will do, their responses are likely to be misleading or valueless. Users also tend to be poor at assessing difficulties which will arise when using requested functions. Problems only become apparent when the system is actually used.

Standard Questionnaires

Standard questionnaires are purchasable or freely available instruments for evaluating a system. They can be used to evaluate operable prototypes, to identify deficits or for quality control on live systems.

User evaluation of the system is carried out in accordance with set criteria. Common standard questionnaires for evaluating software usability include IsoMetrics [Gediga et al. 99], the latest version of which encompasses 75 items, and ISONORM 9241/110 [Prümper 99], which includes a total of 35 questions. Both questionnaires make use of the dialog principles laid out in the ISO 9241-110 standard (see also Sect. 3.6).

ISONORM 9241/110 has also been implemented as an online survey without influencing the results [Richter 99] and thus represents a simple means of evaluating internet applications. Figure 3.15 shows an extract from this online version.

Filling in the questionnaire takes about 20 min. Responses can either be used to produce an overall evaluation of usability (based on the mean score from all questions) or can be analysed at the level of individual ISO principles. This can

Does the software provide support for performing your tasks, without placing an
unnecessary burden on you as a user?

The software ...	---	--	-	-/+	+	++	+++	
is complicated to use.	○	○	○	○	○	○	○	is not complicated to use.
does not offer all necessary functions to efficiently master all given tasks.	○	○	○	○	○	○	○	offers all necessary functions to efficiently master all given tasks.
provides inadequate facilities to automate procedures that recur frequently.	○	○	○	○	○	○	○	provides good facilities to automate procedures that recur frequently.

Fig. 3.15 ISONORM 9241/110 is a standard questionnaire for user evaluation of the usability of
an application. The questionnaire is based on the seven dialog principles set out in the ISO 9241-
110 standard. The figure shows an extract from the principle 'suitability for the task'

Table 3.10 Sample result
of a user survey carried out
using ISONORM 9241/110

ISO principle	x	s
Suitability for the task	4.76	0.88
Self descriptiveness	5.20	0.87
Controllability	4.64	1.05
Conformity with user expectations	4.95	0.96
Error tolerance	4.76	0.97
Suitability for individualisation	3.76	1.22
Suitability for learning	5.48	1.06
Overall ISO evaluation	4.80	0.75

provide an initial indication of potential deficits. Table 3.10 shows a sample
evaluation with mean x and standard deviation s (scale from 1 to 7).

Standard questionnaires for evaluating the user experience of a product are also
available, one example being the User Experience Questionnaire (UEQ) [Laugwitz
et al. 08]. The UEQ covers six factors: attractiveness, perspicuity, dependability,
efficiency, stimulation and novelty.

An important factor with standard questionnaires is the comparability of the data
collected. The fact that all respondents use the same scale allows results to be
consolidated, subjected to statistical analysis and compared. Standard
questionnaires are therefore useful for producing comparisons, should you, for
example, wish to investigate the usability of two different prototypes, results
from different user groups or how a system is evaluated at different time points.

When interpreting results, it is important to be aware that *judgement biases* can
occur when using a questionnaire to perform an evaluation:

- When evaluating software, there is a risk that the assessor will fail to differentiate between individual criteria, and will instead be influenced by their overall impression of the software (*halo effect*).
- The object being evaluated may systematically be assessed too harshly or too leniently (*leniency/severity error*). The reasons for this can vary but may include rejection of the object or personal preferences.
- There can be a tendency to assign a medium score to all questions (*central tendency error*). A strong central tendency error may indicate a poor understanding of the object being evaluated.

Is Usability Measurable?

In practice, two questions tend to crop up – is the usability of a system or product really measurable? And if it is, how can it be measured? A usability measurement could be used to compare different products or perform quality testing. A high usability score measured using generally recognised instruments would also make a good sales pitch. It's not uncommon for publicity to be given to comparisons based solely on expert opinion. Is such an approach sufficient? What form would a more objective instrument for measuring usability take?

Let us recall the definition given in Chap. 1: a human-computer system is made up of the user, the tool (system), the task and the environment. Usability can only be fully evaluated by considering all four components and should therefore take place with actual users in their actual environment. Furthermore, the number of cases must be large enough to allow statistically significant conclusions to be drawn. A good measuring instrument must also meet theoretical quality criteria (see also Sect. 3.7, "Background: Methodological Quality Criteria"). And if we are to be able to say anything meaningful about the magnitude of the measured values (cf. 'the product achieved a score of 6.5'), we need to have sufficient comparison material to allow meaningful interpretation of the results.

Qualitative evaluation techniques such as usability testing and expert reviews deliver important results for development and useful comparisons, and in most cases this is sufficient. They are not, however, capable of *measuring* usability. Suitable quantitative studies involving users in their actual environment are conceivable, but performing them would be laborious and the results would not be comparable across different systems.

The use of standard usability questionnaires represents a promising approach and broadly meets the requirements outlined above. Evaluation of a system is carried out from the user perspective, in the usage context, uniformly, using the same criteria. Questionnaires are tested and optimised for conformity to quality criteria by their authors. **Standardisation** is an attempt to create a basis for comparison between different applications. It should, at least theoretically, be possible to compare results from evaluations of different software products performed by their respective users.

The utility of a comparison between different systems and products is debatable. An interesting practical application would be to use regular user surveys to test the usability of a system over time for quality control purposes. For an online application or mobile app, for example, this could be achieved with little effort using regular online surveys. A decline in the usability score (following a redesign, for example) would flag up a need for action. Some providers are already exploiting this capability and using regular online questionnaires to monitor the usability of their products.

Checklist for Using Questionnaires

- Is a quantitative study necessary and suitable for addressing the question you wish to address or would qualitative techniques (e.g. contextual inquiry, interviews, usability testing on prototypes) be a better option?
- Will numerical values and statistical information help answer your question?
- Are users in a position to answer the questions with their knowledge and experience?
- Can the question to be addressed be packaged into a questionnaire whilst remaining comprehensible and able to be answered within a reasonable period of time? How large is the risk posed by incorrect answers?
- Can statistical analysis meaningfully be performed on the responses and would the amount of effort involved by reasonable?
- Does a custom questionnaire need to be developed or is a suitable standard questionnaire available?

In Brief

Technique	Survey users using a questionnaire
Result	Quantitative data and statistical information on the usability of a system to supplement requirements analysis or for quality assurance
Procedure	Use a standard questionnaire or produce a custom one, conduct the survey and analyse the responses
Work involved	Producing and analysing a small qualitative questionnaire: 5–10 person days
	Conducting and analysing a study using standard questionnaires: 10–20 person days
	Producing and analysing a quantitative questionnaire study: not less than 30 person days
Participants	The client, questionnaire specialists
Scheduling	Analysis: following contextual inquiry
	As an instrument of evaluation: as part of a pilot test or for ongoing quality assurance

Getting a Handle on UX: Planning

4

*We're developing a new product for the mass market. How
much user-centred engineering do we need?
5 kilo should probably do it, sliced would be best. But what
exactly are you planning to do?*

In the previous chapter, we gave a general overview of some of the key user-centred
techniques and how they fit into a user-centred process. To enable these techniques
to be properly deployed, consideration needs to be given to project-specific goals
and risks and the project's constraints (Fig. 4.1). For project managers and the
project team, this means scheduling the required techniques, deploying well-trained
specialists and monitoring progress. This chapter is concerned with how user-
centred engineering should be scheduled within a project.

4.1 Achieving Goals

The emphasis when developing a system or product can vary. Which techniques are
suitable depends on the objectives the project has set out to achieve. It's not unusual
for a project briefing to simply include a blanket requirement for "excellent
usability". If user-centred activities are to be integrated into a project at all, there
need to be evaluable, and ideally measurable, objectives. Below we list a selection
of possible goals:

- to maximise the speed with which users perform their work on the new system
- to minimise the number of steps required and the time needed to perform a
  function
- to minimise the training and learning workload
- to improve the quality of work outcomes
- to increase the number of users who complete the task
- to minimise the number of user errors

© Springer-Verlag Berlin Heidelberg 2014
M. Richter, M. Flückiger, *User-Centred Engineering*,
DOI 10.1007/978-3-662-43989-0_4

Fig. 4.1 The appropriate
user-centred techniques for a
project are determined by the
project's objectives, risks and
constraints

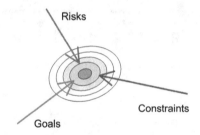

- to reduce the risk posed by misinterpretations and operating errors
- to increase user satisfaction with the product and their tasks
- to increase acceptance of a new product
- to increase the number of users that recommend a product to their peers in social
  networks

If, for example, the management team wants to reduce the time customers spend
in a call centre queue listening to music, employing a system which is efficient to
use can help achieve this. The faster the average call processing speed, the shorter
the waiting time for callers. Reducing the average call processing time is a
measurable goal which can be pursued. It determines which techniques should be
scheduled within the project and what level of resources should be allocated
to them.

4.2   Controlling Risk

A further important factor when planning user-centred activities is risk assessment.
A distinction can be made between project and product risks.

Project risks represent a risk to the successful conclusion of the project. They are
often technical in nature or relate to project politics. Two common project risks
which can be mitigated by user-centred engineering are poor user acceptance and
late discovery of important requirements.

Product risks, by contrast, are risks which could prevent the product from being
used successfully. Human factors often relate to such product risks. Identifying
them helps prioritizing user-centred activities. Some examples:

- Systems with poor usability require more user attention and distract users from
  their actual work. While this risk may be acceptable for an office application,
  appropriate techniques would need to be employed to minimise this risk for a
  new car satnav.
- Input errors can have unpleasant consequences. In a share trading system – if a
  trader inadvertently sells 10,000,000 instead of 10,000 shares, for example –
  they could have serious ramifications. In such cases, input errors need to be
  prevented at all costs.

- The risk posed by an unclear user interface is different when the device under development is a paint mixing machine than it is for a device for dosing medication. Requirements will vary accordingly.

Food for Thought
Are you involved in a project at the moment? Think about the objectives of and risks engendered by that project. Which of these objectives can user-centred engineering help to achieve and which risks can it help to mitigate?

4.3 Constraints

In addition to objectives and risks, the use of user-centred techniques depends on the framework within which the project is taking place. Constraints exert a major effect on how user-centred activities are planned within a project. Contextual inquiry, for example, can only be performed if the project team is in a position to talk to users on site. Below, we give a selection of additional influencing factors:

- How available are users likely to be for observations, interviews and workshops?
- Is the project dealing with in-house or external users?
- How often do users work with the product and how extensive is their specialist knowledge?
- Is development taking place in-house, externally or overseas?
- Does consideration need to be given to people with particular characteristics, such as children, senior citizens, people with poor reading skills or people with disabilities?
- Is any specific hardware or software specified, e.g. devices, multiple monitors, joysticks, voice input, touchscreens, 3D graphics?
- Will the system be used at a particular location?
- At what point in development is the project, how much progress has been made on project objectives, requirements, architecture and the user interface and to what extent are they already fixed?
- What skills in applying user centred methods does the project team currently have? Is there a need to enlist outside consultants and can they effectively be incorporated into the team?
- What corporate guidelines, corporate design specifications and standard procedures need to be taken into account?
- What development process will be used?

4.4   Some Planning Examples

Based on objectives, risks and constraints it is possible to identify:

- what the most appropriate user-centred techniques are
- at what point in time they should be employed
- how much work is likely to be involved
- which personnel with which skills need to be deployed

The following section illustrates this point on the basis of three sample projects.

Agile Development of an In-House Data Processing System

Focus	Efficiency and fitness for purpose
Users	About 700 trained, specialist in-house users who will work with the system intensively
Usability goals	To increase staff productivity; excellent integration into modified processes; to optimise working practices; an efficient user interface; mostly on-the-job training
Project risks	Poor acceptance; lots of remedial improvements; too much time, money and resources spent on development
Product risks	Reduced staff productivity; increased training and support workload
Project status	The (unofficial) project team is working on a project proposal. The team will later comprise 18 people, 8 of them software developers
The process	Following approval of the project proposal, agile development over five releases in two teams

The following techniques will be employed:

- *Contextual inquiry* will be used during the period prior to producing the project proposal in order to identify areas for improvement and any critical factors relating to the current working environment. This information will then be used to adjust the crude business process model. It will also be used on site, during development, in order to obtain detailed information for forthcoming iterations.
- *Storyboards* will be used to document the shared vision for the project proposal and communicate it to management. They will be updated during development to help induct new team members and keep stakeholders in the loop. They will later be used as summaries and introductions during training.
- *User stories*, in a rough form, will be used in the lead up to producing the project proposal to plan the first release. During development, user stories will be added, refined and reprioritised on an ongoing basis. User stories will be used to initiate discussion of user objectives.

- *Scenarios*, based on case studies, will be used to run through new process steps and thereby refine and validate user stories. Scenarios will also be used to produce specific information for the user interface design process. During testing, they will form the basis of test cases and usability testing tasks.
- *UI mock-ups* will be created to determine required functionality and information content (in conjunction with relevant departments) for implementing upcoming user stories.
- *Usability walkthroughs* will be used to check the basic UI concept, prototypes and product increments during development.
- A *project style guide* will be used as a reference work for detailed UI design during development.
- *Usability testing* will be used as part of the acceptance process for releases and selected iterations and for optimising important aspects of the UI during development. It will also flag up any points which need to be given particular emphasis in manuals and training.
- *Questionnaires* will be used once the system has gone live to check that usability goals have been met and again after multiple maintenance updates.

For the procedure outlined above, the project team will need to consider the following points:

- Data processing systems are generally characterised by having lots of exception cases. These typically become apparent only on considering specific examples. Cases which the system fails to take into account mean extra work for users. If too little consideration is given to actual cases, the risk is that users will not be provided with adequate support for the peculiarities of the actual working environment, leading to a fall in quality and productivity.
- The team should involve users in the project wherever possible. It should integrate individual users into the project team, should involve others through occasional participation in surveys and testing, and should keep all users up to date by providing regular information on goals, progress and planning. This ensures that staff starts to prepare for the essential change early on in the process and therefore improves acceptance.
- Ideally, an agile team will take care of all activities from process optimisation through to testing. User-centred engineering and interaction design are part of the team's role. Staff should therefore possess the relevant skill set or be trained by specialists. Usability specialists and interaction designers can advise several teams, deal with any larger issues and provide specialist knowledge.

An Amazing New Digital Gizmo for the Consumer Market

Focus	Simplicity and attractiveness
Users	Consumers from a range of different age groups, both technically minded and complete beginners and from any cultural background
Usability goals	The device should be able to be used immediately with no training; good design; manageable number of features; simple to operate
Project risks	New, relatively unfamiliar technologies; many and varied requirements need to be reconciled
Product risks	High support costs; excessive hotline load; poor sales figures; damage to the company's image
Project status	The product manager has specified a feature set, defined the framework for the project and identified the target group. A specification document for the project team has been produced
The process	Market analysis, concept, iterative development, preparation for mass production, manufacture, launch

The characteristics of an amazing digital consumer gizmo (e.g. a personal video recorder) necessitate a quite different approach to that for an in-house data processing system. The heterogeneity of the user group is particularly challenging. A digital gizmo is simpler than a data processing system from a functional point of view, but involves highly specialised hardware. The following techniques will be employed:

- *Contextual inquiry* will be used for market analysis, to complement market research. The focus would be on problems with existing products and the situations and context in which such products are used.
- *Personas* and *scenarios* will be used during market analysis and the concept phase to model and record users and processes and will be used to sharpen the focus on the target audience and prioritise potential features.
- *UI prototypes* and *usability walkthroughs* will be used during the concept and development phases to define and optimise the product features and user interface (e.g. over weekly iterations). They will also be used to illustrate possible hardware variants and alternative interactivity options, to test them with users and to exclude complex features or hard to grasp concepts and further optimise successful features.
- *Use cases* will be used during the concept phase to identify, refine and update functional requirements.
- *Usability testing* will be used for testing prototypes at the end of a phase and for testing the product prior to launch.

For the procedure outlined above, the project and product managers will need to consider the following points:

- In contrast to an in-house information system, information required for user-centred activities needs to be gathered from a range of different sources. This could, for example, involve using market research to identify relevant cultural factors, such as fashion trends, preferences, etc. Other important information sources could include local distributors and the company's customer service department. Contextual inquiry is also useful for addressing selected questions pertaining to usage and context.
- The product needs to strike a balance between range of features and ease of use. A user-centred methodology can be used to critically examine the benefits of each new feature for the target group and look at how it is used, before it is implemented in the product.
- Users experience software and hardware as a single unit. The device should be presented and evaluated as a single unit from day one.
- Alongside functional factors, emotional factors, aesthetics and design are also important and can be crucial in deciding whether a product is a success or failure.

When It's a Matter of Life and Death

Focus	Safety
Users	Trained professionals with extensive further training
Usability goals	To ensure that incorrect operation does not have serious adverse consequences; to minimise rates of user error; to maximise the quality of achieved outcomes; to make it hard to miss or bypass key steps; to ensure operation is efficient
Project risks	Requirements imposed on the development process are demanding; conditions imposed by legislation and by licensing bodies need to be adhered to; quality standards need to be complied with
Product risks	Accidents could occur, with serious consequences for people, the environment or property
The process	Analysis, concept, development, test phase, manufacture

Products requiring a very high level of safety are used in many fields, including medicine, the car industry, air traffic control and industrial systems. Accidents can occur as a result of operating errors, carelessness or safety measures being actively bypassed ('human failure'). A user interface designed to maximise safety will reduce such accidents, sometimes even at the expense of ease of use and efficiency. Nowadays, for example, drug containers are designed so that they are hard for small children to open. Similarly, to avoid the risk of an inattentive user skipping a critical input field, best practice is to ensure that no default value is assigned to that input field. The following techniques might typically be employed:

- *Contextual inquiry* will be used during the analysis phase to achieve a detailed understanding of and document trained behaviours and the design of existing systems. Environmental and any other critical factors, such as noise, stress, teamwork and behaviour during adverse events, also need to be investigated.
- *UI prototypes* will be created during the concept phase to develop a user interface compatible with technical processes.
- *Usability walkthroughs, expert reviews* and *usability testing* will be applied during the concept and test phases to test the system with users. It is essential both that the design measures employed do actually achieve the aim of improving safety and that the user experience as a whole is satisfactory.
- *Usability testing* will be used during the test phase to validate the system in a usability lab and check the quality of work performed with the system. It will also be used during field testing to analyse incidents in order to identify areas where usability may be inadequate.
- *Incident analysis* will be used to collect and analyse information on safety-related incidents occurring during operation and examine whether applying user-centred measures might be able to deliver improvements.

For the procedure outlined above, the project manager will need to consider the following points:

- A 100 % approach is required. Most optimisation measures are able to achieve a measurable improvement with little effort. In the case of critical risks this is not sufficient. Something as apparently minor as an incorrect default value or an incorrect label on a button can massively increase the likelihood that a particular risk will materialise. Every detail is important.
- 99 % safety is the maximum achievable. It is impossible to completely mitigate all product risks. Everyday life in all its diversity will always throw up unforeseeable situations. A safety-oriented approach therefore places the emphasis on recording and analysing safety-related incidents. Systematic analysis of such incidents from a user perspective helps a project team implement the right improvements in the next version of a product.
- Usability engineering alone is not sufficient – where the level of risk is high, risk management needs to take a broad approach, using measures such as emergency scenarios, user training and certification, incident analysis, etc.
- There are often additional usability standards to be considered in safety-critical environments. In the medical technology sector, for example, relevant standards include IEC 60601-1-6 [IEC 10] and IEC 62366 [IEC 07]. In both of these standards, user involvement is mandatory.

4.5   Involving Users

Many user-centred techniques require the participation of qualified users. This imposes additional tasks on the project team.

Recruiting Users

Recruiting users can be a difficult undertaking. Project teams will often have to recruit users themselves. The following points need to be considered:

- Before conducting any study, think about what characteristics the recruited users should have and check that this requirement is fulfilled.
- Ensure that the recruited users span a wide range of characteristics and abilities.
- Discuss the involvement of in-house users with their superiors.
- For external users, consult with the marketing and sales departments and ensure that confidentiality is properly managed.

Over the course of a large project, a project team will generally involve a whole series of different users. Building a user database will dramatically simplify user recruitment over time.

A detailed treatment of user recruitment and user involvement can be found in [Courage et al. 05].

Rewarding Users

It is appropriate to reasonably reward users. For external users, this usually means giving them money, vouchers or gifts. For in-house users, the esteem of their co-workers is often the best reward. This means employing these users productively and recording and responding to their suggestions and criticisms. It is the project manager's job to keep the involved users up to date on the progress of the project.

Anonymity and Confidentiality

Statements made by users must remain anonymous and be treated as confidential. In an interview situation, analysts may sometimes be exposed to negative comments. Analysts may also observe errors and transgressions. In terms of data protection, the following points need to be considered:

- Participants in a study need to know how the data collected will be used and how anonymity and confidentiality will be preserved.
- Statements recorded by a project team should be anonymised.
- The user's consent needs to be obtained prior to making video or audio recordings. Clarify whether you are permitted to retain recordings and for what purposes they can be used. A simple written consent form is shown in Fig. 4.2.
- Make sure you comply with data protection legislation. This sets out rules for handling personal data.

Information about the usability study

Thank you for agreeing to take part in this usability study for *[name of the organisation]*. Your cooperation is helping ensure that *[name the product]* are better tuned to customer needs. *[The product]* main purpose is to *[give a quick summary of what the product is]*. The focus of the study is *[explain quickly the focus]*.

The usabiliy study will roughly work as follows [brief overview over the study]. You can terminate your participation at any time.

For analysis purposes, the test sessions will be recorded on video and audio. The full recordings will only be analyzed by the project team and once analysis is finished, the recordings will be deleted. Quotes and observations from the session will be handled anonymously: the project team stores such data only by a randomly assigned participant number.

Consent to video recordings

☐ I consent to the full video recordings being saved for later analysis by the project team until the project team finishes the analysis.

☐ I also consent to video segments being used for internal purposes (e.g. montages for presentations to developers and managers).

Signature: Place, Date:

_____   _____

Fig. 4.2 Example of a consent form for the use of video and audio recordings. Please note: Depending on your country's laws and the concrete investigation, you might need additional or even different information on such a consent form

Involving Users Is Project Marketing

All contact with users is an opportunity to explore their fears and concerns and to talk to them about the benefits the product can offer. User-centred techniques are therefore an excellent means of improving user acceptance. This is, however, conditional on the project team engaging with any criticisms or concerns voiced by users. Never forget that *not* talking to users sends out its own message.

4.6   Tricky Situations

Hopefully you should now be champing at the bit to put all this into practice. Sometimes, however, practice can bring you back down to earth with a bump. It can be a hard landing, but there's rarely any permanent damage. In this section, we present a few tricky situations which often crop up in practice and look at ways of dealing with them.

User Representation

In large corporations, **user representatives** may be a permanent fixture of project teams. This is an excellent idea in principle – they are familiar with the field in which the application is used and are able to clarify key points rapidly.

The difficulty in practice is that user representatives are often tasked with defining requirements for the new user interface. But user representatives are not methodologists, systems analysts, user interface designers or software architects. They are rarely in a position to specify an appropriate solution. They may omit core requirements and push their own personal preferences, which are not in the interests of the users they represent. Their role may also cause them to gradually shed the impartial user perspective and they may lose the ability to view the system from a user point of view. The problem tends to be more marked in companies in which staff from commercial departments work full time as user representatives – and are therefore no longer actually users.

Should such a situation arise, the project manager has a key role to play. It is their job to introduce a methodology and to put together a project team with the requisite expertise. Ideally, they will put together an effective team of user representatives. This team should consist of experienced users, span a wide range of specialities and it should perform the following tasks:

* deliver information on user and commercial needs
* answer any technical questions
* facilitate access to users
* check that the system works correctly from a technical point of view

This team comprises the interface between the development team, users and specialists. It shares responsibility for ensuring that user needs are correctly identified. To fulfil this interface function, user representatives should help conduct contextual inquiry, help develop personas, scenarios and storyboards, assist with user interface prototyping and recruit participants for usability testing. In order to perform these tasks successfully, user representatives will require appropriate methodological support.

Users Are Nowhere to Be Seen

Some projects are impeded from accessing users. The result is that analysts miss out on a key source of the kind of information required to develop a usable solution. Where this occurs, the following secondary sources may be useful:

* local distributors
* hotline and support
* training personnel
* training materials and operating manuals

- service personnel
- competitor products
- available literature
- available information about users within the company, from sources such as marketing and market research
- customer contact at trade fairs and exhibitions

Techniques such as personas and scenarios help ensure that what knowledge is available to the project team is used in forming the product vision and that hidden assumptions about users and the application are exposed, allowing a shared understanding to be achieved.

For a business, it can be beneficial to make collection of such information a part of the company culture, thereby establishing a constant line of communication with users and customers. Service engineers could, for example, be explicitly tasked with collecting information about users visited and this information used in future product development.

When Time and Money Are Short

At the start of this chapter, we argued that user-centred engineering within a project should be planned and deployed principally on the basis of business objectives and product risks. In practice, however, time and money are usually limited. Budgets rarely offer scope for a methodology adapted to these objectives and risks. In Chap. 5 we will talk in some detail about the trade-off between cost, time, quality and functionality. Where higher quality is essential – where there are significant product risks, for example – there is no way around using the right methodology; anything else would simply be negligent.

If, on the other hand, the key issues are minimising time to market and a limited budget, you need a process which eliminates the worst usability issues at minimum cost. Some years ago, Nielsen coined the term *discount usability engineering* for this approach [Nielsen 93]. His argument was that, in simple situations, it was possible to achieve a great deal with simple, low-cost techniques and that a simplified approach was more likely to be applied in practice than a more comprehensive, but also more laborious, methodology. A simplified approach might take the following form:

- minimal analysis of usage context – a few on site user observations and interviews rather than detailed contextual inquiry
- lo-fi prototyping of key usage scenarios
- iterative testing and improvement using simple usability walkthroughs with users
- expert reviews based on usability principles or checklists

A Watertight Specification?

Where development of a new solution is outsourced, the ground rules for development are set out by the contract between the client and manufacturer. Particularly in the case of competitive tenders, contracts will frequently contain, in addition to prices, deadlines and quality, detailed specifications for functionality and the user interface. Such a tight framework leaves little scope for improvements once the contract has been signed. Changes are instead largely limited to the cosmetic. If functionality, information or processes do not match user requirements, changes can be made only with great difficulty – coming to an agreement and making contractual changes consume large amounts of time, money and goodwill on both sides.

In a contract situation, the key to ensuring that a planned product achieves the required level of quality for users is the phases leading up to the contract being signed. The client should pay close attention to the following points in particular:

- Analysis, modelling, specification and user evaluation-related techniques should be performed before the contract is awarded.
- The client needs to plan user-centred activities and mobilise the expertise required to perform them.
- The contract needs to specify how user interface design work will be divided between the parties. The contract can also specify how any costs arising as a result of incorrect assumptions or a lack of information on usability-related factors should be apportioned.
- The specification should not only include elaborated use cases, but also a basic user interface concept which has been tested with users and, if required, UI prototypes and style guides.

An entirely different approach consists of *not* fully specifying the product and instead striving to work closely with the manufacturer. Rather than a comprehensive requirements specification, the client sets out project goals and the framework for the project and defines the process. The manufacturer and client work together in applying user-centred techniques. The close collaboration allows both parties to exploit their mutual strengths. If the client has little experience with user-centred techniques, it can take this into account in choosing a suitable contractor to ensure that it has access to the expertise required.

4.7   "It's Carl's Job"

Who is responsible for UX? In practice it varies. Often no-one is responsible. As a result, the UI developer tinkers a little with system usability, the software architect is keen to let you know what he thinks and someone from the commercial side pipes up with their preferences. This kind of approach leaves UX largely to chance or means that it is not considered at all.

Sometimes, however, someone – we'll call him Carl – is given explicit responsibility for UX. Unfortunately Carl is working alone, has no back up and spends all

Table 4.1 Roles involved in user-centred engineering for software or product development

Product manager	Release planning and product roadmap
	Collecting market feedback
	Delineation from competitor products
	Pricing strategy
	Defining sales channels
Risk manager	Identifying product risks
	Defining measures related with the human factor
Project manager	Scheduling user-centred activities
	Promoting awareness of usability and UX
	Procuring the necessary expertise
	Recruiting users for workshops and usability testing
Analyst/requirements engineer	Analysing and describing users and context
	Analysing user-oriented project objectives and risk mitigation
	Identifying and modelling appropriate requirements
	Producing initial user interface designs
	Evaluating the results with users
	Reconciling contradictory requirements
Commercial units	Adaptation of user organisation, processes, operating procedures and workplaces
User interface designer	Designing a functional and aesthetically pleasing user interface
	Optimising the user interface
	Applying style guides
Software architect	Identifying architecture-critical requirements
	Designing a suitable architecture
Developers	Implementing the user interface
Usability test supervisors	Scheduling usability testing
	Specifying test objectives
	Conducting and analysing usability tests
Technical writer	Compiling the help system and operating manual

his time fending off client requests, users' fixed ideas and the software developer's technical preferences.

User-centred engineering is a way of achieving specific goals and reducing risk. It's no use the designer coming up with an appropriate user interface if the software architect chooses an excessively slow architecture and the software developer codes incomprehensible error messages. If such aspirations are to be met, lots of different people have to play their part. Table 4.1 gives an overview of which roles are responsible for which activities.

This lengthy, but by no means exhaustive, list shows just how many different roles influence the usability of a new product or system. Carl may be responsible for UX, but in reality that responsibility is shared by everyone involved in the project, including the client and managers. Good user-centred engineering therefore involves moderating, mediating and exercising good communicating skills, and rarely happens in monastic silence.

A User-Oriented Strategy: Company-Wide UX

5

Equipped with a knowledge of key user-centred techniques, with a good plan in your pocket and the right people on board, your new project kicks off. You aim to finally produce a really genuinely usable product. But things don't go quite according to plan. The budget for user-centred activities is cut, a board meeting signs off new functionality and you've spent the last week feeling like you're talking to a brick wall. In short, you find yourself caught up in the organisational grind of every large corporation

The previous chapters showed how user-centred techniques can be integrated into software or product development projects. This chapter will talk about:

- how UX can be positioned company-wide
- how you can get the departments and people involved in a user-centric process to work together
- strategic aspects of user-centred engineering

This chapter can also be shown to your boss!

5.1 User-Centred Engineering as a Feedback Loop

Establishing a user-centred approach within a company generally means getting rid of some fixed ideas and perspectives. At first glance, bringing customer advisors and developers together for a workshop or spending half a day at a user's workplace may appear unconventional. These activities nevertheless provide insights which save significant time and money and help produce better results.

The goal of user-centred engineering is to produce solutions which are perfectly tailored to users. This requires that:

- information on users, tasks, goals and on the context is systematically fed into the development process

© Springer-Verlag Berlin Heidelberg 2014
M. Richter, M. Flückiger, *User-Centred Engineering*,
DOI 10.1007/978-3-662-43989-0_5

Fig. 5.1 User-centred
engineering creates a
feedback loop between users
and development. This loop
should be as direct as possible

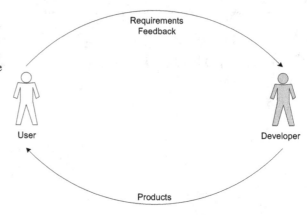

• technical possibilities, limitations and constraints are fed back to users in a
  comprehensible format

From an organisational point of view, this means nothing less than creating a
feedback loop between users and development units. User-centred techniques can
help achieve this, as illustrated in Fig. 5.1.

This view of user-centred engineering in an organisational context liberates us
from considering data collection, user interface design and usability testing in
isolation. Criticism – the latest test report from the usability lab being waved
under the developer's nose – is replaced with a constructive approach. User-centred
engineering brings together the two groups essential to the development of usable
solutions – users and the development team.

The challenge now is to create the conditions required to achieve this feedback
loop. The following sections illustrate three approaches to positioning user-centred
engineering within a company: building a user-centred process, introducing user
interface design standards and tools and making a user-centred approach part of the
company culture.

5.2   Building a User-Centred Process

From an organisational point of view, user-centred engineering operates at the
intersection between the commercial and technical sides of a business. Its objective
is to capture user requirements and, to the extent allowed by technical possibilities
and other limitations, feed them into the development process. To deliver usable
solutions over the long term, businesses need to establish a development process
which incorporates an appropriately timed feedback loop between the commercial
and technical sides of the business.

To provide user-centred activities with the requisite gravitas, it is important that
suitable roles and deliverables are incorporated into this process and that essential
resources (in terms both of time and budget) as well as skilled employees are

provided. In one large company, for example, 'usability engineer' has been defined as a project role. Its responsibilities include supporting the development team in implementing user-centred techniques and producing a basic user interface concept as part of the specification.

There is little benefit in introducing theoretically rigorous rules which fail to achieve acceptance. User-centred activities have to be adapted to the actual existing development process. We consider the following points essential:

- *Business analysis and requirements engineering:* User-centred techniques need to be applied at the point at which commercial or customer-led requirements are being identified, analysed and transformed into specifications or proposed solutions. This is where the course towards a usable solution is charted. Later in the process, the best you can hope to achieve is to adjust that course. Going out of the building and into the environment of your future users is mandatory!
- *An iterative approach:* An iterative process should be employed, in which requirements and specifications can be visualised, tested with users and commercial units and adapted if necessary. If there is a formal release process or specifications have to be signed off by departments, wherever possible these iterative activities should take place beforehand. Close cooperation within the team helps this process.
- *A common, precise language:* To achieve a usable solution, users, business units, departments and developers need to develop a shared understanding. This cannot be achieved through formal, abstract descriptions alone. Example-based techniques such as scenarios, storyboards and user interface prototypes help to promote coherence during product development. The user interface is the common language shared by these various groups and enables them to work together effectively.

Checklist for Adapting Your Development Process

- *Methodology:* What user-centred techniques are most useful and during which project phases?
- *Deliverables:* User-centred engineering applies specific results and models to get at solutions and to document outcomes. What results and models do you need? Should these be combined with, produced in addition to or replace existing deliverables?
- *Tools:* Appropriate tools can be useful for producing informal, visual or prototype-based results (see Sect. 3.4 for an overview of UI prototyping tools). How can you benefit from existing tools and what new instruments do you need to introduce?
- *Feedback loop:* User-centred engineering analyses, interprets and elaborates proposed solutions and tests them with users using an iterative process. Where can feedback loops be incorporated within your company?

- *Roles and activities:* A user-centred process gives rise to new activities and new project roles. Who in your company can adopt these roles? How does the team work together?
- *Principles:* User-centred engineering builds on certain principles (cf. Chap. 7). On what principles is the development process in your company based? Might they be antagonistic?
- *Expertise:* User-centred engineering needs additional skills and expertise. Is the company able to provide projects with skilled people?

5.3   Creating a Common Language

Corporate Style Guides

The chapter on user-centred techniques showed how user interface storyboards and UI prototypes can be used to share requirements between the commercial and technical sides of a company. You have also been introduced to the use of style guides as an important tool for developing uniform user interfaces (cf. Sect. 3.6). In all of these cases, the user interface serves as a common language between those involved in a project. From an organisational perspective, corporate style guides represent the dictionary and grammar of this common language, in that they specify designations and usage rules for user interface elements. This kind of standardisation can improve the long-term consistency and quality of the user interfaces produced by a company.

Developing a corporate style guide is particularly advantageous where a number of similar applications aimed at the same user group, serving a similar purpose and using similar technologies are being implemented. This allows standardised user interface elements to be used in different projects. By contrast, in the case of very different applications or rapidly changing technologies, developing and updating a corporate style guide can be very arduous.

The work involved in agreeing a corporate style guide should not be underestimated. It is often necessary to reconcile requirements from a range of different projects and reduce them to the lowest common denominator. In addition numerous other factors – ergonomics, technical feasibility, corporate design, aesthetics, etc. – all need to be considered.

Corporate style guides should certainly not be viewed as compelling strict (and sometimes blind) adherence to a set of rules. A good style guide enables applications to be produced more rapidly and more easily. Style guides only realise their full potential when, through the use of good examples and other aids, they promote a shared understanding and the sensible application of rules. The following section describes two such aids.

UI Prototyping Tools and Components

The ability of people to miss each other's meanings when discussing something on an abstract level never ceases to amaze; likewise the misunderstandings that are cleared up the moment someone gets out a piece of paper and jots down a quick sketch for a user interface. What works at the micro level is also useful in the context of larger organisations – using user interface sketches to visualise requirements helps avoid misunderstandings. This process can be facilitated by using the following aids:

Prototyping tools provision user interface elements defined in a corporate style guide for use in producing an initial prototype (see also Sect. 3.4). The simpler these tools are, the more prepared less technically-minded people will be to put their thoughts and ideas down on paper. Element collections for simple drawing tools or existing office applications can be used as building blocks to piece together user interfaces and have proven to be a useful tool for this purpose. Figure 5.2 shows a Microsoft Visio®-based tool for producing simple user interface prototypes. The predefined UI elements are corporate style guide-compliant.

Alternatively, defined UI elements can be made available to developers in the form of pre-programmed components. Such components make it easier for developers to comply with style guide rules and improve the quality of the user interfaces produced. Naturally, as with any engineering activity, the effort involved needs to be carefully weighed up.

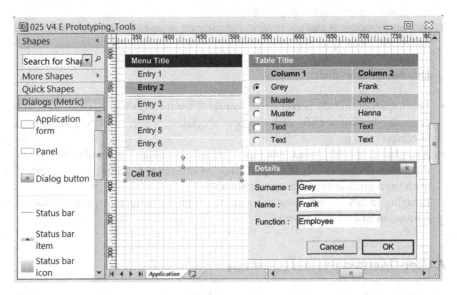

Fig. 5.2 A simple UI prototyping tool allows requirements to be visualised in the form of GUI prototypes. Such tools deliver better user interface quality and consistency across multiple projects

A combination of style guides, prototyping tools and UI components is a fine asset to achieve a user-centred process:

- Being consistent in your designation and use of UI elements ensures continuity in the process of taking the system from specification through to implementation. This facilitates communication and understanding between users, commercial units and developers.
- The specification shows what is technically feasible and is comprehensible to non-technical staff. This enables commercial units to formulate their requirements to take account of technical constraints and to present these requirements visually using initial sketches.

5.4   Establishing a User-Oriented Company Culture

A Dedicated UX Team

For companies with a large number of development projects, it can be worth forming a dedicated UX team. Having expertise in-house offers a range of benefits:

- Experts can help establish user-centred techniques as a permanent feature of the development process and help cultivate a long-term user-oriented mentality by means of internal marketing and training activities.
- A UX team will gradually build up the specific subject and industry knowledge required for user-centred engineering.
- In-house specialists can get involved in projects at an early stage, even before a budget has been agreed.

   Disadvantages include:

- The impartial outside perspective, so useful for user-centred engineering, will gradually be lost – even with the best specialists a degree of 'organisational blindness' sets in.
- Acceptance is often lower than with external specialists. Internally, presenting the user's perspective is often perceived as criticism; hearing the unvarnished truth from outside agents is more palatable.
- Bringing in UX experts does not guarantee the desired user experience, as the discussion in Sect. 4.7 shows.

A User-Oriented Business Strategy

Customer satisfaction, ease of product use and efficient processes are generally high on the list of most businesses' strategic objectives. References to UX in strategy papers and vision statements are increasingly common. Often absent, however, is

Fig. 5.3 Whenever a product is developed, a trade-off has to be made between quality, development time, product functionality and resources and costs. UX is a quality criterion and strategic measures should therefore be taken to ensure that it is maintained

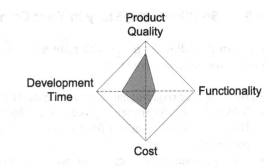

any reference to planning or activities aimed at helping to achieve these strategic objectives.

UX is a quality criterion which can be improved by employing user-centred methods during the development process. It is for the management team to define the extent to which this objective should be prioritised and what resources should be assigned to pursuing it. Figure 5.3 illustrates the interdependencies which need to be considered – a trade-off always has to be made between product quality, functionality, development time and cost.

A market leader, for example, may consider it essential to be first to market with a product with specific functionality and acceptable quality, and will accept the increased costs that this involves. It is, however, impossible to optimise all four of these factors at once. If what you need is to thrash out an application with broadly scoped functionality quickly, it should be no surprise if quality suffers in the process.

A focus on quality is essential if user-centred activities are to be accorded sufficient priority. Once this focus has been set, user-centred engineering can make a major contribution to business success, promoting enduring customer enthusiasm and providing internal users with genuinely efficient applications.

A company can go as far as giving user experience a strategic weight and establish strong leaders that safeguard this quality against other interests, for example a marketing division mainly copying the competitor's features or an over technical R&D department.

Food for Thought
Does your corporate vision reflect your customers' fundamental needs? Is your mission statement based on your users' fundamental problems or is it more technology-driven?

Google has a ten-point company philosophy, which it publishes on its website (www.google.com). The first of these ten points is "Focus on the user and all else will follow." What is your company's guiding principle?

5.5   So What's the Story in Your Company?

Consider the following points with respect to your company. Think about a recent project you were involved with:

- How are user requirements fed into the development process?
- Which people, departments, processes and instruments are involved?
- How is feedback obtained from users consolidated and distributed within the company?
- How satisfied have users been with the results? Is this information even available?

Assess the strengths and weaknesses of the chosen approach. In what areas could selectively embedding user-centred engineering in the company culture improve this?

Food for Thought
Consider the following, real-life examples in the light of the above points. Do any typical patterns emerge?

Example 1

A major bank's internal software development department is developing a specialised application for customer advisors. Commercial requirements are identified by user representatives and collected by a special unit of business analysts. The analysts produce specifications and pass them on to the developers in the form of documents. The company's development process involves having specifications checked and signed off by relevant departments prior to implementation. There is no direct communication between the development department and commercial units. The first customer advisors see of the new application is when it is launched. Acceptance of the new solution is extremely poor, customer advisors largely continue to work with the old system.

Example 2

A centralised department within a public sector organisation is responsible for defining and introducing new IT solutions for roughly 40 local offices which have direct customer contact. Regular meetings are held between the heads of the local offices and the head of the centralised IT department to collect requirements. These requirements are documented and the majority outsourced to external IT service providers. Two or three people who previously worked in a local office are employed within the central department and provide expertise on business cases and telephone support to the local offices. Feedback from local offices varies; the solutions produced are far too complicated.

Example 3

A mechanical engineering business has an R&D department responsible for machinery development. The company has an international clientele with some significant cultural differences. The product manager formulates requirements for new product lines in conjunction with the marketing department and records these in a specification document. Requirements are determined on the basis of feedback from distributors and competitor features. During development projects, machinery, control systems and control panels are specified and developed separately. Project teams obtain initial customer feedback at trade fairs and from selected salespeople at marketing events. The machinery integrates well into customer production processes, but is difficult to use and barely comprehensible even to trained staff.

Points to Watch

It often happens that the project team and users are not able to communicate directly. For a new product, there may simply not yet be any users, or it may be that users are difficult to pin down. However, decision-makers frequently impose separation and barriers for business reasons, with corresponding consequences for communication:

- *Physical distance:* Software and product development is moved to cheaper locations as a cost reduction measure, resulting in a separation from the company's actual business activities and complicating communication channels.
- *Cultural hurdles:* In addition to physical distance, there may also be language barriers and cultural differences.
- *Business boundaries:* Technical services are outsourced to third parties and their suppliers. Doing business internationally also involves working with distribution partners and service units. Their processes, management and business goals may vary.
- *Organisational distance:* even within a company, users are often far removed from developers organisationally. Where intermediaries such as user representatives, business analysts and superiors perform coordination tasks, information still has to flow through several different bodies.
- *Methodological gaps:* Business analysts record requirements in abstract specifications, market research departments condense findings on target groups into statistics and superiors summarise user needs. The consolidation of user requirements may be necessary, but inappropriate methods prevent important information on users from finding its way to developers.

That's Life: Examples from Actual Practice 6

It seems to me that some have many tools and few ideas,
others have many ideas and no tools.

(Denis Diderot)

In this chapter we present four real-life projects which illuminate the use of the user-centred techniques described above in software and product development. You may find that some of the challenges have a certain ring of familiarity about them.

6.1 Case Study 1: User-Centred Requirements Clear the Air

For a major manufacturer of humidification systems we applied a user-centred approach in requirements engineering and development of a new application for calculating humidification products. This enabled an efficient, integrated application with a minimum of effort.

Profile

Users	Sales staff at various overseas offices
Product	Software for specifying humidification systems, including a product catalogue
Usability goals	To make the sales process efficient and effective, to achieve consistency across all product families
Project phases	From creating the vision to implementation
Techniques	Personas and scenarios, contextual inquiry, UI storyboards, UI prototypes, use cases, usability walkthroughs

© Springer-Verlag Berlin Heidelberg 2014
M. Richter, M. Flückiger, *User-Centred Engineering*,
DOI 10.1007/978-3-662-43989-0_6

Initial Situation

Humidification systems are used in many different fields. They are used to create a pleasant, healthy atmosphere in offices and shopping centres, to improve hygiene in hospitals, prevent potatoes from rotting in food stores and ensure that concrete has the correct humidity for optimal curing. Various technologies and components for ensuring the correct humidity are available, making use of techniques such as evaporation and vapour injection.

When specifying a humidification system for a quote, sales staff use software applications which help them select the right components and the right size of unit. For larger projects, responsibility for designing humidification systems generally rests with external planners retained by the customer.

At the outset of the project, the programs used to specify systems were complex and unwieldy and a different program was used for each product family and technology.

Challenges

- It was not initially clear whether the software would be used solely by sales staff or whether it would also be made available to outside planners.
- The new application will be used in the company's overseas offices throughout the world. The overseas offices use different languages, have different local requirements and differ markedly in terms of their size, the sales process and the systems with which they need to connect.
- Different specification software and product catalogues are used for different product families. One of the challenges is to produce a unified application which incorporates the company's entire product portfolio whilst avoiding unnecessary complexity for the user.

Procedure

Initial workshops with the client were directed towards analysing the sales process with respect to the new solution. Close examination of potential user groups showed that the needs of sales staff and the needs of outside planners were sufficiently different that they could not both be addressed by the new application. A key step, therefore, was to delineate the target group. The project managers decided to develop the initial version of the software for sales staff only.

Participants from five different overseas offices came together for a user workshop aimed at developing realistic personas and scenarios for using the new software. The scenarios were a useful starting point for optimising support for a typical sales process and were used to delineate and focus functionality for users. Sharing ideas between participants also helped demarcating the scope of the new software from existing systems currently used in the overseas offices. For purposes such as generating and storing written quotes, and ordering products and components from the parent company different systems were in place.

The next step involved a visit to a typical overseas office. Sales staff provided information on their workflows, ranging from the first telephone contact with the customer through to producing a written quote. Some critical steps were observed in action on site. The team collected valuable information on workspaces, processes and the environment in which the software would be used. The so identified user requirements were summarised in a vision document.

To obtain feedback from representatives from relevant departments the team produced user interface storyboards. This process involved a number of short cycles. The storyboards showed the process for specifying components for humidification systems and provided an initial impression of the basic GUI concept for the application. Figure 6.1 shows several iterations from the first drafts to the final user interface.

The team used these storyboards and the documented requirements to produce a functional GUI and architecture prototype, permitting further cycles of feedback on

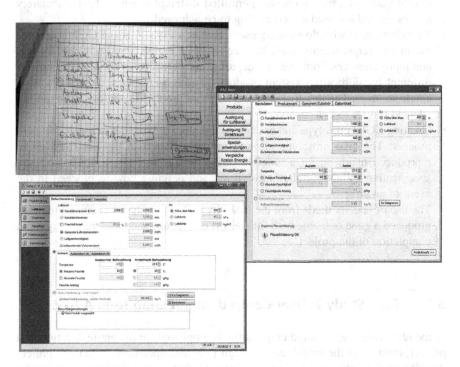

Fig. 6.1 *Top*: Basic GUI concepts have been visualised using simple hand sketches. The drawing shows some of the parameters required for calculating air humidity and how they are integrated into the planned sequence of dialogues. *Middle*: The revised dialogs were contextualised using a detailed storyboard. Mock screenshots were produced using MS Visio®. *Below*: Screenshot of the final application

the basis of a tangible object. At the same time, use cases were specified to formally describe and, over a series of iterations, firm up details of functional processes.

The GUI prototype meant that the team was soon in a position to obtain user feedback by conducting usability walkthroughs, in which sales staff used the prototype to process a fictional customer enquiry. The results of the walkthroughs allowed to further optimise the prototype.

Implementation of the application was then carried out based on the prototype and a specification consisting of use cases and additional requirements.

Benefits and Summary

- Actively delineating the target group early in the project proved to be a big help in focusing the product vision. This was an important step for avoiding unnecessary functionality and a prerequisite for good usability.
- Early involvement of users from a range of different overseas offices and joint development of usage scenarios permitted different needs to be immediately addressed and a shared understanding to be achieved.
- Visualisation of workflows using user interface storyboards and GUI prototypes meant that requirements could be checked at an early stage. Product managers and representatives from relevant departments were able to see how the various different humidification system product families were being integrated into a single solution. The iterative approach allowed proposed solutions to be rapidly adapted to user requirements.
- Creating a GUI prototype and use cases in parallel proved to be a highly efficient process. The GUI prototype allowed individual steps in the use cases to be reproduced hands-on on a tangible object, whilst use cases rounded off the specification by adding alternative flows and defining how to proceed in the event of an error.
- The use of lean methods from the usability and requirements engineering fields produced a good outcome with little effort or expense and led to relatively rapid completion of the project.

6.2   Case Study 2: User-Centred Engineering from A to Z

In the ideal case, user-centred engineering is employed for the entire duration of a project, right from the initial idea through to actual operation. In the rail project described below, the project team applied user-centred techniques throughout the development process. This ensured that the software delivered to users was able to meet the demanding requirements imposed by their work.

Profile

Users	Operating staff at a number of different rail companies
Product	Bespoke software for dealing with disruptions to rail traffic
Usability goals	Rapid communication with minimum errors in demanding situations
Project phases	Vision, concept, two-stage implementation
Techniques	Contextual inquiry & design, storyboards, UI prototyping, usability walkthroughs and testing, role plays, feedback questionnaires

Initial Situation

In the event of a fault on the rail network, within minutes, a large number of people will spring into action to resolve the fault and minimise the effects on customers and trains. This requires that large volumes of detailed information and decisions are communicated between these people – information such as the status of the disruption, what needs to happen to affected trains, how passengers can be transported to their destinations with as little delay as possible, and more. For major events – say, for example, a stretch of track is out of action completely – prepared emergency plans are implemented.

Telephone-based communication, as of today, is redundant, error-prone and costs valuable time that could be better spent dealing with the actual event. The new system is intended to ensure that information reaches users precisely and reliably, ensuring that it can be dealt with rapidly and correctly.

Challenges

- When a fault occurs, users are fully occupied with its resolution. This means that superfluous information and any difficulty in operating the software need to be minimised.
- Fault resolution requires many years of experience and high levels of expertise, something which only long-serving staff possess. Involving these staff in the project was therefore essential.
- Users rely on the information provided by the system. Incorrect or incomplete information could have costly consequences.

Procedure

With support from a usability engineer, a team of users and departmental experts used requirements and user-centred techniques to put in place the foundations for

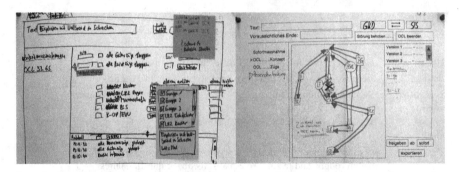

Fig. 6.2 Requirements for the new software were elaborated in sketch form in the course of workshops involving users, technical experts and usability engineers. The sketches show basic concepts for dealing with faults on the rail network efficiently (©Swiss federal railways, 2009)

development. The team used paper mock-ups to outline ideas and possible approaches. Figure 6.2 shows some of the sketches produced by the team in a series of workshops.

The team also analysed communications during a fault. This involved installing video cameras and asking staff to switch them on in the event of such a fault. The video recordings and subsequent interviews delivered valuable insights and helped to sharpen the product vision. It turned out, for example, that dispatchers were receiving and forwarding large volumes of information, leaving them little time to actually deal with the fault. Removing the need for dispatchers to perform this information coordination function became a key focus for the new software.

With a clearer vision, it became possible to consolidate and work out the details of the many different approaches to a solution. In particular, this meant producing a storyboard. This provided a first visual representation of the new system and included many key details of the user interface and connected systems, whilst placing it in the ordinary work context. This enabled benefits and concerns to be discussed with staff and managers. The project team also examined what effects potential solutions were likely to have on processes. Role plays helped to assess what process changes were required and get an initial feel for feasibility.

Finally, an interactive UI prototype was produced, illustrating a large portion of planned features. Once the utility of the system had been adequately demonstrated by conducting usability walkthroughs, this prototype formed the basis for development together with a requirements document.

For the development phase, the team was expanded to include software developers and an interaction designer. User-centred techniques were employed on a continuous basis. The team used mock-ups to elaborate details of the user interface, whilst selectively employing usability testing to obtain the confidence and knowledge required to resolve difficult design problems. A mobile usability lab was used for tasks such as optimising keyboard entry speed. The iterative approach enabled the project team to deploy an initial version before project completion. This enabled forthright feedback from day-to-day operations to be fed back into the development process. Figure 6.3 shows a screenshot of the finished software.

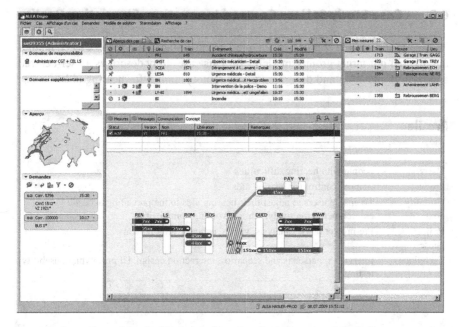

Fig. 6.3 Screenshot of the final software for rail operating personnel, including an overview panel, fault reports, fault resolution and a schematic (© Swiss federal railways, 2009)

Benefits and Summary

- Experts in day-to-day operations – i.e. future users – were involved at all stages of the project. Essential knowledge pertaining to fault resolution was available within the team. Having a team with this composition provided a solid base from which to build useful software.
- The use of user-centred techniques was not restricted to a single usability expert; they were employed by the project team as a whole. In particular, users within the project team were trained in the use of such techniques. This allowed all team members to contribute to a good usability.
- The fact that usability was systematically considered from the outset of the project ensured that implemented components possessed excellent usability. During the actual development usability testing was applied selectively, and thus efficiently, with the principal aim of optimising particularly challenging aspects of the system.
- It proved impossible to recreate the complexities of day-to-day operations in the kind of artificial setting offered by a usability lab. In order to tackle any shortcomings, it was therefore necessary to launch an initial version of the new software early in the project.

6.3   Case Study 3: User-Centred Innovation: Simulating Reality

How can user-centred engineering help in the early stages of a project when neither the product nor target groups are defined? This case study describes a user-centred approach to planning and designing a new remote control for hearing aids.

Profile

Users	People with hearing difficulties
Product	Remote control for hearing aids
Usability goals	To enable users to adjust their hearing aids to the prevailing acoustic environment effectively, whilst avoiding complexity
Project phases	Pre-project phase, analysis, vision, concept, requirements
Techniques	Interviews, personas and scenarios, interaction design, UI prototyping, usability testing

Initial Situation

Most modern hearing aids have various settings to allow users to adjust them for the prevailing acoustic environment. People with limited hearing are, for example, able to adjust the volume to their needs and switch between programs designed for specific acoustic environments. Depending on the model, hearing aids are adjusted either directly via controls on the hearing aid or via a special remote control which the user carries with them.

Currently available remote controls provide a wide range of functionality, but are too complicated for many users. A hearing aid company therefore decided to design a new range of hearing aids with a novel, much simplified remote control. This new remote control would be small, light and very easy to use. Hearing aid user requirements for such a remote control were, however, largely unknown.

Challenges

- The project was at the early innovation stage, and the nature of the future product was still largely up for grabs. Target groups, scope of functionality, size and shape, technology, key functions and many other points remained to be determined, and a wide range of different opinions and ideas for potential solutions had been put forward within the company.
- The user group – hearing aid users – is difficult to qualify and has a range of different needs. The majority of hearing aid users are older people with

progressive hearing loss. Older people are more likely to not accept complex functions and operating procedures. Factors such as mobility and range of activities undertaken can, however, vary widely. The result is that the frequency with which users adjust their hearing aids and how they do so varies.

- The job of the new product will be to adjust hearing aids to the situation in order to optimise hearing. Acoustic environments are hard to observe. It is impossible for an outside observer to deduce what users will deem to be an appropriate setting.
- It is hard to put the acoustic experience and other key concepts relevant to hearing aid operation into words. Achieving a shared understanding among project participants was therefore extremely important.

Procedure

The first phase involved taking stock within the company to collect relevant information on hearing aid users and how hearing aids are used and operated. This principally involved interviews and workshops with stakeholders and specialists, including product managers and the R&D, marketing and market research departments. Audiologists are responsible for adjusting the hearing aids in direct customer contact. They were able to provide useful information on user needs. Other sources were customer feedback on existing products, results from market research and user studies, competitor products, and business and project goals. The results were summarised into a vision document.

The next step involved interviews in which hearing aid users were sounded out about their needs with regard to controlling their hearing aid and remote control use. Figure 6.4 shows such an interview situation. The results from these workshops and interviews were used to create and prioritise personas and scenarios for the new remote control.

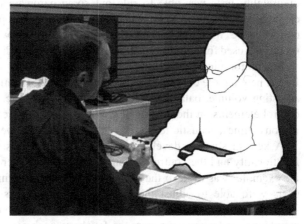

Fig. 6.4 A user demonstrates how he has to switch on his remote control to change hearing programs on his hearing aids. Qualitative interviews with users bring problems with today's applications to light and focus on the real user needs

Fig. 6.5 Simulation of a usage setting with the new remote control: In this usability test scenario users had to adjust their hearing aids while watching TV at home and talking to others

To further define the size and shape, control elements, key functions and overall functionality of the new remote control, the team undertook tests of various versions and hardware prototypes with users. Short usability testing cycles were used to obtain results, exclude solutions which proved to be problematic and refine the interaction design.

For this purpose an in-house prototyping platform was developed, which used video and audio recordings to simulate a range of different hearing environments and provide users with a realistic impression of a fully functional hearing aid remote control device. The prototyping platform offered the ability both to examine existing use cases relating to the operation of todays hearing aids and to try out scenarios for future hearing aid lines which did not yet exist as such or had not yet been technically implemented. Figure 6.5 shows the setup with the prototyping platform and a video sequence which was used for the tests.

Usability testing was carried out with hearing aid users from potential target groups. The prototyping platform placed users in realistic acoustic environments where they were asked to interact with various prototype remote controls. The first set of usability tests was able to rule out some hardware options involving control elements which proved to be comparatively difficult to operate in actual use. Other options were well received by users. Figure 6.6 shows some of the hardware prototypes used for usability testing, featuring a range of different key configurations.

The prototyping platform not only allowed to explore different hardware options for the new remote control, but also the mapping of functions (switching programs, adjusting volume, balancing different input sources etc.) to physical buttons and control elements on the new device. While simulating real conditions, factors like response times, acoustic feedback and other variables were also varied.

A key question in developing the new control was the relationship between functionality and the control options offered by the user interface. One objective, for example, was to keep the number of keys to a minimum whilst ensuring that users were able to adjust the most important settings easily. Usability testing showed that users found the device difficult to use both when there were too many keys, and when there were too few keys, each performing multiple functions.

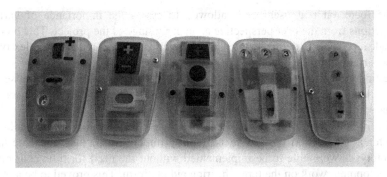

Fig. 6.6 Users evaluated a range of different hardware prototypes during usability testing. Physical control elements, key functions and the functionality and interaction concept of the remote control were all varied

Fig. 6.7 The end product – a new, simple, efficient hearing aid remote control with a small number of keys and an optimised operating concept (© Phonak AG, 2012)

An easily understood interaction concept with optimised key functionality was identified after some more iterations. Figure 6.7 shows the new remote control at launch.

Benefits and Summary

- A user-centred approach can deliver important insights from the user's perspective even during the innovation phase and thereby provide important pointers, in conjunction with the technical framework and strategic considerations, for designing a new product.
- Participants in the project used personas and scenarios to uncover implicit assumptions about users and usage situations. This facilitated discussion and created a shared understanding of the product vision.

- The focus on real user needs allowed to assess the importance of various functions from the user perspective at an early stage of the project. This process made it possible to delineate the planned functionality and reduce complexity for users right from the beginning.
- Testing various versions in iterative usability test series helped to minimise risk by allowing less successful solutions to be ruled out early in the project and enabling successful versions to be further optimised.
- The in-house prototyping platform developed for usability testing allowed different interaction designs to be rapidly implemented. Functional, testable prototypes were able to be implemented without the need for time-consuming development work on the target hearing aid platform. This proved to be a major advantage. It allowed mature interaction concepts for the new remote control to be developed early in the project and to be tested with users.

6.4   Case Study 4: Discount Usability Engineering

It is not always possible to involve a usability engineering expert throughout the course of a project. We therefore wish to present a case study where a short involvement produced a big effect.

Profile

Users	Cutting machine operators, programmers and service staff
Product	Control panel for an industrial sheet metal cutting machine
Usability goals	To combine simplicity and a wide range of uses
Project phases	Concept, elicitation of requirements
Techniques	Personas and scenarios, UI prototyping, design workshops, use cases

Initial Situation

A manufacturer of cutting machinery was well positioned in the premium sector and wanted to launch a new product to penetrate a new market segment. The new product would be designed such that it would be affordable for small companies with two to three employees. The machine would allow these companies to cut small batches of sheet metal parts of almost any shape – lamps, cogs, ventilation grills, brackets, and many more – out of a single piece of sheet metal. Significant development work had already been carried out, and the current challenge was to define the graphical user interface for the control panel. Figure 6.8 shows a sketch of a cutting machine control panel.

Fig. 6.8 A sketch of the
planned control panel
illustrates the combination of
physical controls and a GUI

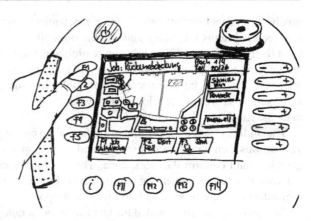

Challenges

- The international nature of the customer base for the machine dictates a degree of distance from users both geographically and organisationally, with all communication with customers occurring indirectly via local distributors.
- The control panel consists of both a GUI and hardware, which forms part of the machine. The way the machine operates influences control panel design and vice versa.
- The budget provided for just a few days of usability engineering work.

Procedure

Usability engineering work focused on capturing requirements. Simple personas helped to give the project team a better understanding of the target audience. These personas were based on information obtained from local distributors using questionnaires and on individual interviews with service technicians and with training staff who made occasional customer visits. These personas helped to dispel many preconceived ideas. The project team discovered that, rather than the oft-cited rice farmers with a little on-the-job training, they were in fact dealing with well-educated graduate engineers. In keeping with this, the personas showed that the planned strict division of roles between cutting machine programmers, who set up and configure jobs on the machines, and operators, who then execute the pre-configured tasks, was not an appropriate model.

During requirements elicitation, the team also produced a user interface storyboard. This gave a detailed account of a typical scenario for machine usage.

This provided the materials required for a workshop with the goal of defining the control panel user interface. Achieving this, however, meant considering the production process as a whole – from defining a job, receiving and feeding in raw materials, starting and monitoring production, to removing finished parts and waste and dealing with faults. Interest was high among all sections of the workforce involved in development, with senior mechanical engineering staff, electronic engineers, systems engineers and marketing staff all invited and arriving eager for a lively discussion. The workshop participants used the personas to go through the scenario step by step. A polystyrene model of the planned machine formed the set, with the user interface storyboard providing the script. The results were surprising – as well as developing many facets of the control panel concept, the machine itself was also simplified.

The findings from the workshop were firmed up by the project team. The revised version was then used to organise a second workshop to explore as yet unresolved questions and confirm the work done. The resulting scenarios and user interface storyboards made documenting requirements simple. Use cases and sketches of the user interface were used in addition for this purpose.

The usability expert provided the team with methodological support, led the two workshops and provided regular feedback on mock-ups produced by the team. The resulting specification was then implemented.

Benefits and Summary

- On an industrial manufacturing machine, hardware and potential production processes impose stringent constraints on the control panel user interface. Usability discussions were strongly focused on processes and hardware, resulting in a sleek and simple design. This had the side effect of triggering improvements to the machine and processes.
- The division of work between different roles and the level of user education is defined by machine buyers and their staffing structures. Personas helped to introduce these two points into the discussion. They also brought the target audience into sharper focus and helped to dispel various preconceived ideas. The result was that processes on the control panel were made simpler and more direct.
- User interface prototyping with paper as well as with the development environment, allowed the team to implement multiple iterations in a short period of time. The costs involved in making changes according to personas and production processes and dealing with feedback from the project team and usability expert could be kept to a minimum.
- The project did, however, lack a feedback loop from actual users. Detailed analysis using contextual inquiry and usability testing with users would certainly have unearthed many other important issues, but would also have required a far larger budget for user-centred activities.
- The chosen compromise was right for both manufacturer and customers. The former was able to produce a control panel which offered a good level of usability compared to competitor products; the latter received a high-performance machine at a good price, which was easy enough for their staff to work with.

Flashback: Principles of User-Centred Engineering

7

So this, then, was the kernel of the brute!

(Johann Wolfgang von Goethe)

User-centred engineering pursues a specific philosophy. This chapter summarises a few key points in the form of five core principles. You may find it helpful, in a quiet moment, to revisit these five principles and use them to check that you are headed in the right direction.

7.1 Identifying the Question: A Goal-Oriented Approach

Think back over the techniques and concepts presented in this book. We have repeatedly stressed the importance of defining your questions and goals to guide your methods:

- Contextual inquiry is not just going to the users and watch them doing their tasks. It is guided by the unanswered questions to which we are seeking answers. Analysts prepare themselves intensely by generating hypothesis and writing down the open questions they wish to have answered.
- How personas are characterised varies according to whether the emphasis is on quality of work, efficiency, safety or on specific user goals with the planned product.
- Examining the question you wish to address can help identify which approach to prototyping will help you achieve your objective. Is the intention to clarify requirements, to come up with a basic user interface concept, to optimise the user interface or to produce a specification?
- How and when questionnaires should be used depends on the question your study is intended to address.

© Springer-Verlag Berlin Heidelberg 2014

M. Richter, M. Flückiger, *User-Centred Engineering*,

DOI 10.1007/978-3-662-43989-0_7

Fig. 7.1 A simple tool for use in a workshop setting for identifying questions to be addressed and scheduling planned user-centred techniques

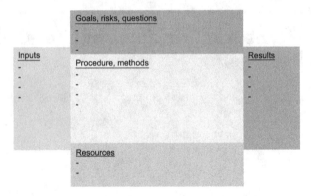

All the techniques we have discussed should be built around a well-thought out question. Figure 7.1 shows a tool for use in a workshop setting for developing such a question. Participants write down goals, intended results and add any inputs, techniques and required resources.

7.2   Context: Designing for Reality

By definition, usability does not depend solely on the product itself, but is the result of the interaction between users, tools, the task and the environment. User-centred techniques therefore aim to take account of the actual usage context:

- When conducting contextual inquiry, analysts visit users and observe them at work.
- Personas and scenarios are used to feed the context into the design and development processes.
- Storyboards show the product in the environment in which it is used.
- Usability testing involves running through realistic scenarios.

A product is not a closed system; it is inextricably linked to the context in which it is used. To ensure that a planned solution fits into its environment, you need to see how it interacts with that environment.

When applying user-centred techniques the project should perform a reality check on the applied methodology, see Fig. 7.2. Is the context completely ignored, simulated or even fully real? What about users, tasks and the product? Creating a situation as realistic as possible usually means to invest more time. Iterations take longer and fewer feedback cycles are possible. So does the project team make good choices between being realistic and having quick iterations?

To get reality into the project is not a simple matter and project teams need quite some creativity to achieve this without losing speed in iterations. Get creative and ask yourself over and over again: What could we do to get closer to the real thing?

Fig. 7.2 Rethink your methodology: the closer you get to reality the more reliable you can expect the result to be but the longer your iterations tend to be

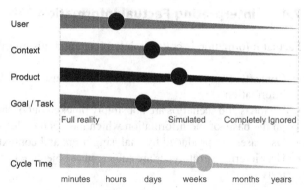

7.3 Partnership: Involving Users Constructively

Partnership means treating users as experts in their field and taking into account their wishes and needs. Users are familiar with the details and peculiarities of their day-to-day work and are the ultimate arbiters of the new system's practical utility.

- Contextual inquiry is used to gain familiarity with how the experts perform their work in situ.
- Storyboards, UI prototypes and style guides create a language which is comprehensible to both users and developers and enables them to work together.
- Usability testing involves exposing the project team's work to systematic criticism from users.
- Questionnaires enable a system to be evaluated from the user perspective.

Project staff and users form an interdisciplinary team and together address a selected question. This ensures that their collaboration is constructive.

7.4   Interpreting Factual Information

Factual information is collated, interpreted and this interpretation then examined:

- Contextual inquiry and questionnaires are used to collect and evaluate factual information.
- Personas and scenarios are not simply plucked out of thin air; they are elaborated on the basis of the information which has been collected.
- Use cases are produced by analysing users and context.
- User interface prototypes are subjected to objective testing by means of usability tests.

When discussing software, the discussion should be as dispassionate as possible. Members of the project team should examine and if need be revise any preconceived opinions they may hold. Let the collected facts speak for themselves, listen attentively and design software which is in keeping with these facts.

7.5   Modelling and Collecting Feedback

Developing a useful solution means creating, evaluating and optimising designs and models:

- Contextual inquiry takes as its reference points existing systems and work processes. It is not simply a question of asking users for their ideas. Even in initial interviews, sketches, prototypes and comparable products can create a link with the user's own experience.
- Personas and scenarios model user needs and requirements. These are then worked up into storyboards and user interface prototypes which provide the user with a realistic impression of the planned solution.
- Use cases provide a representation of a new system's planned functionality. Their accuracy is refined on the basis of feedback from participants.
- User interface prototypes mirror planned processes from the user perspective.

In user-centred engineering, an understanding of modelling is essential. A product which can be used effectively and efficiently is not created off the cuff, but requires several different feedback cycles. The goal of modelling is not creating a model itself, but gaining a deeper understanding from different perspectives and getting feedback about the planned solution. Modelling is about communication.

Food for Thought
Think about an existing project. What would you need to change to apply the five principles outlined above to the methodologies used in that project?

Outlook: Related Fields

8

In the final chapter of this book, we offer an overview of some related fields and topics. Drawing up precise boundaries showing where one field ends and other fields begin is impossible and is not our intention. This chapter instead aims to illustrate the various strands within the profession, the direction in which the discipline is developing and to indicate some headings under which to find more information on specific topics.

8.1 Accessibility

The accessibility speciality is concerned with how technical systems can be made accessible to people with disabilities or particular limitations. Accessible technologies are particular important for public systems such as ticket machines, government websites, information systems and internet applications.

A key principle in the field of accessibility is that of equality. People affected by visual, cognitive or motor impairments should be broadly enabled to use technical systems in exactly the same way as people who do not have a disability. Modern technology is helping people with such impairments lead independent lives. Electronic publications, for example, enable blind and partially sighted people to consume written media. Online applications avoid the need for trips to banks and supermarkets. Many countries have extensive equality legislation.

The process of standardising web technologies has also given rise to accessibility standards. These include the Web Content Accessibility Guidelines 2.0 [W3C 08], which have been an ISO standard [ISO 12] since 2012. Among other things, adherence to this standard ensures that fonts are freely enlargeable and that content can be outputted using Braille readers and voice output systems. Especially public sector websites are required by law to be accessible.

© Springer-Verlag Berlin Heidelberg 2014
M. Richter, M. Flückiger, *User-Centred Engineering*,
DOI 10.1007/978-3-662-43989-0_8

8.2   Interaction Design

Interaction design defines the options for controlling a system, system behaviour and how it responds to the user. The field of interaction design focuses on elaborating and designing interaction concepts for digital products and applications. As well as designing the functional user interface (user interface design); it focuses on a good user experience in a wider sense, encompassing the overall experience when using the product. User-centred engineering, interaction design and user interface design are therefore closely coupled and drawing a clear dividing line between them is difficult. User-centred techniques are used to define required functionality, information content and processes and to test them with users. Interaction design involves incorporating user needs into specific designs for the user interface. User interface design includes implementing the concepts on the target platform.

The issue of interaction design has been touched on several times in the preceding chapters.

- In Sect. 3.4 we showed how prototypes can contribute to producing a basic user interface concept, optimising control elements and elucidating a design.
- Section 3.6 gave a summary of guidelines and rules for the visual design and layout of a specific user interface.

Interaction design involves the following principle elements:

- knowledge of good design and design processes, with an emphasis on interactive products, e.g. from the graphic and industrial design disciplines
- creative design techniques and activities, with consideration given to the feeling to be conveyed by the product
- a detailed knowledge of the user interface technology used

The type of user interface is significant here. Although the user-centred techniques used with different technologies are very similar or even identical, whether you are developing a data processing system, a mobile device, a control panel for a piece of machinery or a ticket machine makes a big difference to the user interface design. Consideration needs to be given to the following points:

- input and output devices and methods, such as pens, gestures, mice, keyboards, monitors, touchscreens, keys and in-built displays
- the control elements and interaction principles used
- the structure and layout of the user interface
- factors such as ergonomics, graphic design, industrial design, technical feasibility, corporate design and aesthetics

Recommended works on interaction design include [Cooper et al. 07] and [Buxton et al. 12].

8.3 Security and Usability

The field of IT security is concerned with protecting systems and the information they process from unauthorised access. Traditionally, IT security experts have primarily been concerned with technical measures such as encryption, authentication procedures, anti-virus protection, firewalls, etc.

Input from usability specialists is, however, increasingly being sought in relation to security. A system can only be secure if its users employ security features correctly. We are all familiar with examples of everyday incorrect usage – sending out confidential documents by email in unencrypted form, re-using the same password over and over again, opening potentially dangerous emails, etc.

For security features to actually get used, they have to be simple and efficient, and not get in the way of our work. A technical improvement in security which unreasonably impedes teamwork, user mobility or efficiency will simply be bypassed.

Consequently, the IT security field is paying increasing attention to how people behave when using technology. User-centred techniques help provide an understanding of users' actual objectives and behaviour. As a result, there has been a jump in publications dealing with the interdependency of security and usability. A detailed treatment of the subject can be found in the book *Security and Usability* [Cranor et al. 05].

8.4 Web Usability

After the internet boom at the end of the last millennium, many companies started to realise that websites only achieve the desired effect if they offer good usability. A host of publications containing procedures, guidelines, tips and tricks for user-friendly website design appeared (see also Sect. 3.6). Web usability became almost a synonym for good web design.

There are a number of specific factors which affect website usability.

Websites generally display large volumes of information which visitors have to navigate. How users find their way around a website is therefore a key issue. Consequently, developing a comprehensible, clearly laid out *information architecture* is essential.

Although graphics and imagery have long been an important component of web design, text remains the major medium for conveying information and content. Web usability therefore also deals with the display and preparation of text for web use.

Websites are where two opposing interests collide – the visitor's desire to find information and content and the marketing department's wish to communicate a corporate identity. A feel for effective text and image-based communication is therefore essential for web usability. There is a large body of literature on web usability and web design. We recommend the book from [Krug 14].

New mobile technologies and the increasing prevalence of broadband connections mean that over the last ten years the web has undergone another major shift after the transformation from a university knowledge network into a commercial information platform. Multimedia content, collaboration and community platforms are the trends now transforming our everyday lives and social behaviour. Dissemination of information is now becoming mixed up with social interaction and interactive applications. The web usability field faces some interesting new challenges.

8.5   Mobile User Experience

A new generation of mobile devices and technologies boasting intuitive operating concepts has heralded a new era of information technology. Mobile products are changing our everyday lives. There are a range of new concepts to be considered when designing mobile applications and services.

Simple Access, Anytime, Anywhere

People have hankered after mobile access to information since the 1990s, when, equipped with a laptop, a modem, an expensive data tariff and a great deal of patience, steadfast users were able to work on the go. The real change is not the *fact* of being able to answer emails, surf the web and edit our documents from anywhere; the real revolution is the *simplicity* with which this is now possible and the market penetration that it has consequently achieved. Having a smartphone in your jacket pocket is now all you need to be able to comfortably take care of most tasks on the go. As a result, consciously or unconsciously, work and communication now permeate our day-to-day lives. We have gained flexibility and are able to make better use of time spent waiting. We have less need for forward-planning. Mobile applications are also changing our behaviour, and that includes our social behaviour. We are now able to interact via a range of different channels (phone, text, email, the web, Facebook, forums, apps, etc.) as and when required. Work is invading our private lives. This has both positive and negative effects, and these are set to become an important issue for mobile product development.

Selected Functionality

Mobile use of services and products has a further consequence for product and service design. The benefit provided by extensive integration between solutions is declining. Today, functionality is distributed across numerous smaller entities, each of which is used in specific situations. Smart apps and online services for mobile devices are now visibly displacing the large software packages of yesteryear. Consequently, app designers are having to pay even closer attention to underlying

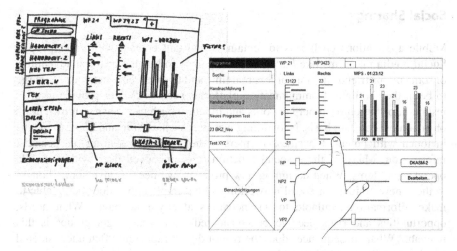

Fig. 8.1 When developing a mobile application, the reduction to the optimal minimum has a major effect on product success. Carefully chosen functionality and interaction design are essential for creating an appropriate mobile user experience

usability issues. Who is the planned target group and what are their needs? In what context and in what situations will the application be used? What features deliver genuine benefit to users in these situations? Selectively reducing functionality of traditional applications to increase their suitability for mobile devices and technologies is a key task when designing successful mobile applications (see also Sect. 1.3, "User-Centred Engineering: Reduction to the Essential"). Figure 8.1 illustrates a reduced user interface for mobile usage.

Location-Based Services

Just a few years ago, service providers were still puzzling over how to make location-based services attractive to users. Today we take it for granted that, thanks to GPS and internet connections, our mobile devices always know where we are and what is around us. Where's the nearest good pizza place? What's that building in front of me? What does the photo I just took show? When's the next train home and is it on time? With the right apps, tasks like these are now trivial. As a result, user expectations tend to be high. When designing a new application, designers need to work out what items of location-based data provide genuine added value and whether and how this data can be used.

Social Sharing

Mobile applications enable us to remain in constant contact with other people. **Social media** platforms like *Facebook* enable us to follow the pictorial adventures of some of our friends in more or less real time and to give free rein to our own urge to be in the spotlight. Communication platforms such as *Twitter* provide us with instant information from our networks and in return push us to share our own news on an almost constant basis. Networking websites such as *Xing* and *Linkedin* put us in touch with potential business partners or help promote sharing of specialist information. Many of these social functions are embedded deep within mobile operating systems. When designing new products, we need to give some thought to these new options for social networking. What implications does being able to make information available to our networks at any time have? What needs, opportunities and risks need to be considered? For what target groups is this relevant? What consequences does the rise of direct, rapid and often unconsidered word of mouth communication have?

There are many more questions which need to be considered in terms of interaction design and implementation of mobile applications:

- What devices will the application run on? What operating systems and **mobile platforms** will be supported? Recent years have spawned a great deal of diversity. The most prominent mobile platforms are Apple iOS devices (such as the iPhone and iPad), Google's Android OS, used on a wide range of devices of every possible shape and size from lots of different manufacturers, and Microsoft's mobile operating system and tablet hardware. Making provision for platform-specific design principles and guidelines requires user interface designers and developers to have a detailed knowledge of the field (see also Sect. 3.6).
- Particularly challenging is the interplay between different channels when planning new services, for example when designing the functionality to be offered by applications which will be available as traditional applications, online services and mobile apps. **Multi-channel** strategies are increasingly important for businesses. Considering a mobile user interface in isolation is not sufficient.
- Mobile devices employing the new capabilities described are enjoying excellent market penetration. New apps are easily accessible to users, allowing them to reach a broad, heterogeneous user base. The flipside of this is that switching to a competitor product is also extremely simple.
- Mobile applications impose high access and data security requirements (see also Sect. 8.3 about the interdependency of security and usability) and raise a range of data protection issues, to which serious consideration needs to be given.

When designing mobile solutions, care needs to be taken to address these and other user needs and requirements. User-centred techniques which involve the usage context and which help users to imagine their environment have an important role to play during development.

We described a similar problem in the case study "User-centred innovation – simulating reality" (Sect. 6.3). With mobile applications, producing a realistic simulation of the future application early in product development provides a range of benefits. This kind of approach is not limited to producing prototypes. It also involves simulating realistic usage situations – e.g. using the application on a train, in a coffee shop, at home, on the way to work, etc. – and running through them with users. This allows a new product to be optimised under realistic conditions, in the course of short usability testing cycles and with a reasonable level of resource use.

8.6   The Ubiquitous Computer

The field of *ubiquitous computing* starts from the hypothesis that the omnipresence of computer technology heralds a new era for the information society. The term was first coined in a paper by computer scientist Mark Weiser [Weiser 91].

Increasing miniaturisation and connectivity mean that intelligent objects are becoming more and more commonplace and are supplanting the paradigm of the traditional desktop computer and all the limitations that go along with it. Numerous examples already exist – computerised building control systems, the fusion of computers, video recorders, hi-fi systems and televisions, media-friendly, internet-connected intelligent fridges, micro RFID chips for labelling objects, mobile devices and applications, smartphones, tablets, etc. In the future it is conceivable that our environment will be filled with large numbers of even smaller computing units.

Weiser was keen that, in addition to the technological possibilities, there should also be discussion of the sociological changes which this new era will usher in. One of the key features of this change is that computerisation of the environment will remain largely invisible and, in contrast to conventional computers, will not require our conscious attention. Information will in principle be available wherever it is needed. It will be accessed naturally without leading to information overload. This will make applications faster, simpler and more intuitive. Information will also be available to people who do not currently have access to the relevant technologies.

There are still a lot of questions hanging over this vision. Issues such as security, privacy and data protection are going to be particularly challenging.

This paradigm shift will also mean changes to the field. Individual, non-standardised device hardware, new ways of interacting, intelligent, thinking systems, and devices which are integrated into the environment will impose a new set of demands on user-centred engineering (Fig. 8.2).

One thing that won't change, however, is that as information technology becomes increasingly integrated into our professional and personal lives, the 'human factor' will continue to play a key role. Analysing and understanding human goals and behaviours will become ever more essential for implementing useful, usable applications.

Fig. 8.2 Intuitive operation, attractive design and situation-appropriate features have resulted in a new generation of mobile applications – and users. Where will the journey lead?

Captain's log, supplemental. How do you turn this darn log off?

Glossary

Agile	The term *agile* designates a set of principles, methods and approaches for improving productivity by reducing bureaucracy and focusing on a small number of key axioms, specifically iterative development, collaboration, incremental improvement and adaptation to changes.
Analyst	A role within the development process. In this book, this refers primarily to people who are occupied with capturing and modelling requirements.
Business modelling	A set of techniques for producing, managing and examining a model of a business system, usually an organisation or enterprise.
Computer	A machine with which you can write almost as fast as you can think. (Umberto Eco)
Context	Also usage context. The environment in which a technical system is embedded, consisting of users and their working practices and the cultural, social, organisational, physical and technical environment.
Ergonomics	The study of the relationship between man and his work, tools and environment.
Evaluation	Designation for the process of assessing a technical system with users.
(G)UI guidelines	Usually fairly general guidelines on the use and behaviour of (graphical) user interface elements.
Human-computer interaction (HCI)	The study of communication between humans and computers.

© Springer-Verlag Berlin Heidelberg 2014
M. Richter, M. Flückiger, *User-Centred Engineering*,
DOI 10.1007/978-3-662-43989-0

Human factors   The field of psychology concerned with human characteristics
                       and behaviour when using technology.

Interaction design   The design of the interaction between the user and system.
                       Interaction design defines the options for controlling a sys-
                       tem, its behaviour and its responses. The field of interaction
                       design is concerned with defining a good user interface by
                       involving users and includes aspects of graphic and indus-
                       trial design.

Iterative approach   The process of repeating a goal-oriented development cycle
                       – from analysis through to evaluation – so that prototypes or
                       components of a new system gradually converge on the
                       desired solution.

Mobile user   The design of the overall experience when using mobile
experience   devices, applications and services.

Mock-up   A dummy version of the user interface which can be
                       evaluated by users and other stakeholders. Can be created
                       using simple media such as paper, cardboard or polystyrene
                       or using electronic media such as graphics programs. The
                       term lo-fi prototype is also used.

Modelling   A simplified representation and illustration of a specific
                       segment of reality for a specific purpose. Modelling is a
                       necessary activity on the road from user requirements to a
                       system specification.

Process   A sequence of actions for achieving a specific goal. Com-
                       monly encountered meanings include information flows and
                       collaboration within a company (business process), user
                       workflows with a specific system (human-system interac-
                       tion), process models for producing applications and
                       products (development process).

Requirement   A required characteristic which a new system needs to meet.

Requirements   A set of techniques for capturing, modelling, managing,
engineering   evaluating and communicating requirements for the devel-
                       opment of technical systems.

Software   Study of and adaptation of computer programs to human
ergonomics   needs and requirements.

Specification	A description of a new solution intended as a template for development. Sometimes part of the contract between the client and manufacturer.
Style guides	Specific visual design and layout rules for a specific user interface. Style guides describe the look and behaviour of user interface elements, depending on the technology employed.
Usability	A measure of the user's effectiveness, efficiency and satisfaction with a technical system.
Usability engineering	The systematic application of methods and techniques with the aim of designing and manufacturing useable systems and products.
Usability lab	A facility specifically set up for usability testing.
Usability principles	General guidelines for user-centred user interface design. Usability principles can be used both to design and to evaluate user interfaces.
Use case model	A model of system behaviour. The most commonly used modelling elements are use cases, actors and relationships.
User	A role within the software or product development process. This role should be filled exclusively by people who may potentially use the new system.
User-centred design (UCD)	Process model which systematically involves users in the development of systems and products.
User-centred engineering	Involving end users with the goal to achieve the desired functionality, usability and user experience when developing new software, products or services.
User experience (UX)	A person's perceptions and responses that result from the use or anticipated use of a product, system or service [ISO 10].
User experience design	Discipline concerned with the design of product or service-related communication with the user in its entirety.

User interface	Also human-machine interface. The user interface encompasses those parts of a system with which people interact directly.
User interface design	Discipline concerned with designing user interfaces on the basis of defined requirements.

Bibliography

[Apple 92–13] Apple. (1992–2013). OS X human interface guidelines. http://developer.apple.com/mac/library/documentation/UserExperience/Conceptual/AppleHIGuidelines/

[Apple 08–14] Apple. (2008–2014). iOS human interface guidelines. http://developer.apple.com/library/ios/documentation/UserExperience/Conceptual/MobileHIG

[Beck et al. 01] Beck et al. (2001). Manifesto for Agile Software Development. http://agilemanifesto.org/

[Beyer et al. 98] Beyer, H., & Holtzblatt, K. (1998). *Contextual design: Defining customer-centered systems.* San Francisco: Morgan Kaufmann.

[Buxton 07] Buxton, B. (2007). *Sketching user experiences: Getting the design right and the right design.* San Francisco: Morgan Kaufmann.

[Buxton et al. 12] Buxton, B., Greenberg, S., Carpendale, S., & Marquardt, N. (2012). *Sketching user experiences: The workbook.* San Francisco: Morgan Kaufmann.

[Cockburn 00] Cockburn, A. (2000). *Writing effective use cases.* Boston: Addison-Wesley.

[Cohn 04] Cohn, M. (2004). *User stories applied: For Agile Software Development.* Boston: Addison-Wesley.

[Constantine et al. 99] Constantine, L., & Lockwood, L. (1999). *Software for use: A practical guide to the models and methods of usage-centered design.* Reading: Addison-Wesley Professional.

[Cooper 04] Cooper, A. (2004). *The inmates are running the Asylum: Why high tech products drive us crazy and how to restore the sanity.* Sams: Pearson Education.

[Cooper et al. 07] Cooper, A., Reimann, R., & Cronin, D. (2007). *About face 3: The essentials of interaction design.* Indianapolis: Wiley.

[Courage et al. 05] Courage, C., & Baxter, K. (2005). *Understanding your users: A practical guide to user requirements methods, tools and techniques.* San Francisco: Morgan Kaufmann.

[Cranor et al. 05] Cranor, L. F., & Garfinkel, S. (2005). *Security and usability: Designing secure systems that people can use.* Sebastopol: O'Reilly Media.

[EEC 90] EEC. (1990). Council directive of 29 May 1990 on the minimum safety and health requirements for work with display screen equipment (fifth individual Directive within the meaning of Article 16 (1) of Directive 87/391/EEC). (90/270/EEC)

[Garrett 10] Garrett, J. J. (2010). *The elements of user experience: User-centered design for the web and beyond.* Berkley: New Riders.

[Gediga et al. 99] Gediga, G., Hamborg, K.-C., & Düntsch, I. (1999). The isometrics usability inventory: An operationalisation of ISO 9241-10. *Behaviour and Information Technology, 18*, 151–164.

[Google 14] Google. (2014). Google user experience principles. http://www.google.com/corporate/ux.html

[IEC 10] IEC 60601-1-6. (2010). Medical electrical equipment – Part 1–6: General requirements for basic safety and essential performance – Collateral standard: Usability. International Electrotechnical Commission (IEC)

© Springer-Verlag Berlin Heidelberg 2014
M. Richter, M. Flückiger, *User-Centred Engineering*,
DOI 10.1007/978-3-662-43989-0

[IEC 07] IEC 62366. (2007). Application of usability engineering to medical devices. International Electrotechnical Commission (IEC)

[ISO 1996–2014] ISO/DIS 9241. (1996–2014). Ergonomics of human-system interaction. ISO 9241:1996–2014

[ISO 98] ISO/DIS 9241-11. (1998). Guidance on usability. ISO/DIS 9241-11:1998

[ISO 10] ISO/DIS 9241-210. (2010). Ergonomics of human-system interaction – Part 210: Human-centred design for interactive systems. ISO 9241-210:2010

[ISO 06] ISO/IEC 25062. (2006). Software engineering – Software product Quality Requirements and Evaluation (SQuaRE) – Common Industry Format (CIF) for usability test reports. ISO/IEC 25062:2006

[ISO 12] ISO/IEC 40500. (2012). Information technology – W3C Web Content Accessibility Guidelines (WCAG) 2.0.

[Johnson 07] Johnson, J. (2007). *GUI Bloopers 2.0: Common user interface design don'ts and dos.* San Francisco: Morgan Kaufmann.

[Kroll et al. 03] Kroll, P., Kruchten, P., & Booch, G. (2003). *The rational unified process made easy: A practitioner's guide to the RUP.* Amsterdam: Addison-Wesley Longman.

[Krug 14] Krug, S. (2014). *Don't make me think, revisited: A common sense approach to web (and mobile) usability.* Berkley: New Riders.

[Laugwitz et al. 08] Laugwitz, B., Held, T., & Schrepp, M. (2008). Construction and evaluation of a user experience questionnaire. In A. Holzinger (Ed.), *USAB 2008, LNCS 5298* (pp. 63–76). Heidelberg: Springer. http://www.ueq-online.org/

[Mayhew 99] Mayhew, D. (1999). *The usability engineering lifecycle: A practitioner's handbook for user interface design.* San Diego: Morgan Kaufmann Academic Press.

[Microsoft 05–14] Microsoft. (2005–2014). Windows user experience interaction guidelines. http://msdn.microsoft.com/

[Miller 56] Miller, G. A. (1956). The magical number seven, plus or minus two: Some limits on our capacity for processing information. *Psychological Review, 63,* 81–97.

[Nielsen 93] Nielsen, J. (1993). *Usability engineering.* San Francisco: Morgan Kaufmann.

[Norman 88] Norman, D. (1988). *The psychology of everyday things (new title: The design of everyday things).* New York: Basic Books.

[Prümper 99] Prümper, J. (1999). Test IT: ISONORM 9241/10. In H. J. Bullinger & J. Ziegler (Eds.), *Human-computer interaction – Communication, cooperation, and application design* (pp. 1028–1032). New Jersey: Lawrence Erlbaum Associates.

[Richter 99] Richter, M. (1999). Online survey as a new method to evaluate the usability of interactive software. In U.-D. Reips, B. Batinic, W. Bandilla, M. Bosnjak, L. Gräf, K. Moser, & A. Werner (Eds.), *Current internet science – Trends, techniques, results.* Zürich: Online Press. http://gor14.gor.de/archive/gor99/tband99/

[Robertson et al. 12] Robertson, S., & Robertson, J. (2012). *Mastering the requirements process: Getting requirements right.* Amsterdam: Addison-Wesley Longman.

[Robson 11] Robson, C. (2011). *Real world research.* Indianapolis: Wiley.

[Rosson et al. 02] Rosson, M. B., & Carroll, J. M. (2002). *Usability engineering: Scenario-based development of human computer interaction.* San Francisco: Morgan Kaufmann.

[Rubin et al. 08] Rubin, J., & Chisnell, D. (2008). *Handbook of usability testing: How to plan, design, and conduct effective tests.* Indianapolis: Wiley.

[Schwaber et al. 91–13] Schwaber, K., & Sutherland, J. (1991–2013). The Scrum guide. http://www.scrumguides.org

[Scott et al. 09] Scott, B., & Neil, T. (2009). *Designing web interfaces. Principles and patterns for rich interactions.* Sebastopol: O'Reilly Media.

[Snyder 03] Snyder, C. (2003). *Paper prototyping: The fast and easy way to define and refine user interfaces.* San Francisco: Morgan Kaufmann.

[Standish Group 94–14] The Standish Group. (1994–2014). Chaos report. http://www.standishgroup.com

[Tidwell 11] Tidwell, J. (2011). *Designing interfaces: Patterns for effective interaction design.* Sebastopol: O'Reilly Media.

[W3C 08] W3C Web Content Accessibility Guidelines 2.0. (2008). http://www.w3.org/WAI/

[Weiser 91] Weiser, M. (1991). The computer for the 21st century. *Scientific American, 265*(3), 94–104.

Further Reading

Goodwin, K. (2009). *Designing for the digital age.* Indianapolis: Wiley.

Holtzblatt, K., Wendell, J., & Wood, S. (2004). *Rapid contextual design: A how to guide to key techniques for user-centered design.* San Francisco: Morgan Kaufmann.

Kuniavsky, M., Goodman, E., & Moed, A. (2012). *Observing the user experience, second edition: A practioner's guide to user research.* San Francisco: Morgan Kaufmann.

Sharp, H., Rogers, Y., & Preece, J. (2011). *Interaction design: Beyond human-computer interaction.* Indianapolis: Wiley.

Wiegers, K., & Beatty, J. (2013). *Software requirements.* Redmond: Microsoft Press.

Zaki Warfel, T. (2009). *Prototyping: A practitioner's guide.* Brooklyn: Rosenfeld Media.

Index

© Springer-Verlag Berlin Heidelberg 2014
M. Richter, M. Flückiger, *User-Centred Engineering*,
DOI 10.1007/978-3-662-43989-0

Printed in the United States
By Bookmasters